FOGS, CLOUDS AND AVIATION

Fog and Cloud

F. Ellerman, photo.

FOGS CLOUDS AND AVIATION

By

W. J. HUMPHREYS, A.B., C.E., Ph.D., Sc.D.

Meteorological Physicist (Retired, Collaborator), United States Weather Bureau; Author of "Physics of the Air," "Weather Proverbs and Paradoxes," "Rain Making and Other Weather Vagaries," "Fogs and Clouds," "Snow Crystals" (with Wilson A. Bentley), "Weather Rambles," "Ways of the Weather," etc.

BALTIMORE
THE WILLIAMS & WILKINS COMPANY
1943

COPYRIGHT, 1943
THE WILLIAMS & WILKINS COMPANY

Published August, 1943
Reprinted March, 1944

COMPOSED AND PRINTED AT THE
WAVERLY PRESS, INC.
FOR
THE WILLIAMS & WILKINS COMPANY
BALTIMORE, MD., U. S A.

I bring fresh showers for the thirsting flowers
    From the seas and the streams;
I bear light shade for the leaves when laid
    In their noonday dreams.
From my wings are shaken the dews that waken
    The sweet buds every one,
When rocked to rest on their mother's breast,
    As she dances about the sun.
I wield the flail of the lashing hail,
    And whiten the green plains under,
And then again I dissolve it in rain,
    And laugh as I pass in thunder.
                  —SHELLEY, *The Cloud.*

PREFACE

This book is for the convenience of those who need a fuller account of the phenomena here described than is given in general works on meteorology. The significance to the aviator of each type of fog and cloud is noted, but not elaborated in detail, since to do so would be both impracticable and useless.

The current international nomenclature and classification of clouds is followed, while the descriptions given are in substance essentially the same as those that have been in use more than half a century. In the main, the text of my former book, *Fogs and Clouds*, has been followed.

The two letters, aa, ab—ca, cb, etc., that are here given with many of the cloud pictures suggest one shorthand method of recording the kinds of clouds observed—the first letter denoting the basic class, the second, the variety. Of course instead of letters one could use figures, symbols or any other distinctive device.

CONTENTS

I	EVAPORATION AND CONDENSATION	1
II	FOGS	19
III	CLOUD FORMS	39
	Cirrus	46
	Cirrostratus	62
	Cirrocumulus	63
	Altocumulus	71
	Altostratus	79
	Stratocumulus	81
	Nimbostratus	82
	Cumulus	91
	Cumulonimbus	110
	Stratus	117
	Special Cloud Forms	120
IV	CLOUD MISCELLANY	154
V	CLOUD SPLENDORS	178

PORTRAITS

Aitken John.................. 13   Howard, Luke............... 43

ILLUSTRATIONS

FIGURE			FIGURE		
1.	Frost smoke..............	22	30.	Altocumulus.............	75
2.	Radiation fog............	24	30a.	Altocumulus, banded....	76
3.	Radiation fog............	25	31.	Altocumulus.............	77
4.	Advection fog...........	27	32.	Altostratus..............	83
5.	Advection fog...........	28	33.	Stratocumulus...........	84
6.	Advection fog...........	29	34.	Stratocumulus...........	85
7.	Advection fog...........	30	35.	Stratocumulus...........	86
8.	Cirrus....................	48	36.	Nimbus..................	87
9.	Cirrus....................	49	37.	Nimbus..................	88
10.	Cirrus....................	50	38.	Cumulus.................	93
11.	Cirrus....................	51	39.	Cumulus.................	94
12.	Cirrus....................	52	40.	Cumulus.................	95
13.	Cirrus....................	53	41.	Cumulus.................	96
14.	Cirrus....................	54	42.	Cumulus.................	97
15.	Cirrus....................	55	43.	Cumulus.................	98
16.	Cirrus....................	56	44.	Cumulus.................	99
17.	Cirrus....................	57	45.	Cumulus.................	100
18.	Cirrus....................	58	46.	Cumulus.................	101
19.	Cirrus....................	59	47.	Cumulus.................	102
20.	Cirrus....................	60	48.	Cumulus.................	103
21.	Cirrostratus..............	64	49.	Fractocumulus...........	104
22.	Cirrostratus..............	65	50.	Fractocumulus...........	105
23.	Cirrostratus..............	66	51.	Fractocumulus...........	106
24.	Cirrocumulus.............	67	52.	Firecumulus.............	107
25.	Cirrocumulus.............	68	53.	Firecumulus.............	108
26.	Cirrocumulus.............	69	54.	Cimulonimbus...........	111
27.	Cirrocumulus.............	70	55.	Cumulonimbus..........	112
28.	Altocumulus..............	73	56.	Cumulonimbus..........	113
29.	Altocumulus..............	74	57.	Cumulonimbus..........	114

ILLUSTRATIONS

FIGURE
58. Cumulonimbus 115
59. Cumulonimbus 116
60. Stratus................... 118
61. Stratus................... 119
62. Billow cloud.............. 121
63. Lenticular cloud.......... 124
64. Lenticular cloud.......... 125
65. Lenticular cloud.......... 126
66. Lenticular cloud.......... 127
67. Lenticular cloud.......... 128
68. Lenticular cloud.......... 129
69. Crest cloud............... 131
70. Crest cloud............... 132
71. Crest cloud............... 133
72. Crest cloud............... 134
73. Banner cloud............. 137
74. Cumulus boa............. 139
75. Cumulus boa............. 140

FIGURE
76. Scarf cloud................ 142
77. Scarf cloud................ 143
78. Tonitrocirrus 146
79. Tonitrocirrus 147
80. Mammatocumulus 148
81. Mammatocumulus 149
82. Tornado or funnel cloud.. 150
83. Tornado or funnel cloud.. 151
84. Tornado or funnel cloud.. 152
85. Snow crystals............. 156
86. Crepuscular rays......... 179
87. Lightning................. 181
88. Lightning................. 182
89. Lightning................. 183
90. Lightning................. 184
91. Rainbow.................. 188
92. Halo...................... 189
93. Corona................... 191

Chapter I

EVAPORATION AND CONDENSATION

> I am the daughter of earth and water,
>   And the nursling of the sky;
> I pass through the pores of the ocean and shores;
>   I change but I cannot die.
> —Shelley, *The Cloud*.

WHERE FROM AND WHERE TO

Everyone knows that rain and snow come out of the clouds, and that every cloud and fog particle is either a water droplet or an ice crystal. Naturally, therefore, one asks where all this endless supply of water comes from; endless, because year after year, century after century, and age after age, rain and snow have descended as they now descend. And where, too, does it all go, this world average of 16,000,000 tons a second? The answers are: It comes from the soil and its vegetation, from rivers, lakes, and the oceans; and to them it returns—an endless cycle of evaporation and condensation.

> The mist and cloud will turn to rain,
> The rain to mist and cloud again.
> —Longfellow.

The first of these processes, namely, evaporation, consists in the change of water (water in this case, though many substances behave similarly) from the liquid, or even solid, state to that of an invisible gas, in which condition it becomes, though always relatively small, part of the air we breathe.

The rate of this evaporation depends on a number of things, the more important of which are:

a. The evaporating surface. The larger the surface the more rapid the evaporation from a given mass or volume of water. It is in recognition of this law that we spread out a drop or even a puddle of water to hasten its disappearance.

b. The temperature of the evaporating water. The higher this temperature the more rapid the evaporation. This is why heating things hastens their drying.

c. The velocity of the wind to which the water is exposed. This explains why roads, for instance, dry so much quicker when the winds are strong than when they are light.

d. The amount of moisture already in the atmosphere. The wash on the clothesline, as every housewife knows, dries provokingly slowly during cloudy, muggy weather.

All the other factors that affect the rate of evaporation, such as density of the air, saltiness of the water, etc., generally are small in comparison with the above, and need not here be considered since it is only intended to make perfectly clear, through our everyday experiences, the wide occurrence and great importance of evaporation.

SATURATION

Although evaporation, as just stated, is so very general there are conditions under which things will not dry, nor bodies of water any longer decrease. Thus even a rather small amount of water in a tightly closed bottle, or other impervious vessel, remains there indefinitely. The space above the water becomes saturated, we say, by which we mean that it gets so charged with water vapor that, under the existing conditions, it can contain no more. At this stage the net evaporation is zero. That is, the amount of the invisible water vapor that now goes back, or condenses, into the liquid stage is exactly equal to that which, in the same time, leaves the liquid surface and becomes invisible vapor. In other words, at this stage, however rapid the interchange between liquid and vapor, the amount of each remains constant.

Numerous careful experiments have determined very closely the exact weight of water vapor per cubic foot say, cubic meter, or any definite volume, when the space in question is saturated at any given temperature, from the boiling point to far below that of freezing. And these experiments show two facts of paramount importance in the formation and dissipation of clouds, namely:

1. The amount of moisture necessary to produce saturation increases rapidly with increase of temperature.

2. The amount of water vapor essential to saturation is not appreciably affected by the presence or absence of the other gases of the normal atmosphere.

It is true that even in technical language we often say that the *air* contains such or such an amount of moisture, as though the presence of the air was essential to the existence of the vapor, or as though the air acted somehow like a sponge in taking up water. But, as explained, this idea is wholly wrong. The only appreciable effect of the presence of the other gases of the atmosphere on the moisture is that of slowing the rate of its spread or diffusion. Temperature and temperature alone, to within a negligible amount, determines the quantity of vapor per any given volume necessary to produce saturation, or, of course, any definite percentage or fraction of saturation.

CONDENSATION

The percentage of saturation produced by a given amount of water vapor may, therefore, as is obvious from the above discussion, be varied by altering the volume it occupies or its temperature, or both; and as rapidly as saturation tends to be exceeded moisture condenses out onto any water-wetable surface or solid that may be present. Thus, the deposition of dew, the formation of hoarfrost, and the sweating of ice pitchers all are examples of condensation owing to passing the saturation point or dew point, as it commonly is called. In these cases just mentioned the temperature of the water vapor and, of course, of the other constituents of the atmosphere, which, however, play no part in the condensation, is lowered through contact with cold objects, and the volume of this vapor, as well as that of the accompanying chilled gases, decreased—decreased because in the open air the pressure remains constant, or nearly so, whatever the degree of cooling.

Similarly, whenever the temperature of the open air passes below the dew point condensation occurs in the form of innumerable water droplets or tiny ice crystals throughout the chilled volume, and thereby produces a fog or a cloud, as determined by location—a fog if on the surface, a cloud if only in mid-air.

The natural processes by which a given body of the atmosphere may be sufficiently cooled to lose a portion of its water vapor by condensation are: (1) Contact with objects colder than itself; (2) mixing with colder air; (3) radiation; (4) expansion.

Condensation as a result of contact cooling is well illustrated, as already explained, by the deposition of dew—the bedewed objects having been cooled by radiation; by the formation of hoarfrost, which occurs under the same conditions, except at a lower temperature, as does dew; and by the sweating, during warm humid weather, of all cold objects. It is further illustrated by the formation of fog, generally light, when relatively warm humid air drifts over a snow bank or other cold object.

The second of the above processes of inducing condensation—that is, the mixing of masses of humid air of different temperatures—is not very effective. Indeed, an accurate calculation, based on the temperature and volume changes and other factors of the problem, shows that while a fog or cloud may be obtained by this process no appreciable amount of rain or snow is likely to result. Layer or stratus clouds at the boundary between relatively warm air above and cold beneath, a phenomenon of occasional occurrence, are at least partially due to mixing, as are also the fogs that so frequently occur over adjacent warm and cold ocean currents.

The third process by which air loses heat, namely, by radiation, probably is of little importance in the production of clouds, since the most chilled portions of free air sink to lower levels and thereby, owing to heating by compression, become even warmer and drier than they were at first. Near the surface, however, where descent and the consequent dynamical warming, as it is called, are impossible, radiation often is very effective in the production of fog.

The last of the cooling processes mentioned above —that is, expansion—is exceedingly effective, and to it is due the great bulk of cloud formation. Now, expansion of the air may be produced either by heating it or by reducing the pressure to which it is subjected. It is the latter process, obviously, and not the former, even though heating generally is the initial cause, that produces the cooling of free air and the formation of cloud. To make these points clear, consider the results when a given mass of humid air is heated, as it often is, over a region warmed by sunshine or otherwise. With increase of temperature it expands and thereby becomes lighter, volume for volume, than the surrounding cooler air. The surrounding denser air then underruns the lighter and lifts it up to higher levels, just as hot air is driven up a chimney. As the warmed air is thus forced up (rises, as we generally but erroneously say) the pressure to which it is subjected obviously decreases in proportion to the weight of the air left below. It therefore gradually expands as it rises and thereby does work, and since the only energy available for this work is the heat of the ascending air, it follows that as its height increases its temperature must correspondingly decrease. As a matter of fact, for air of average humidity, the rate of this decrease is approximately 1°C. per 100 meters (1°F. per

187 feet) increase of elevation up to the base of the cloud, if there be one, in the rising air, and then much less through the cloud. In any event the ascending air attains equilibrium only when it has cooled by expansion to the temperature of the air that finally surrounds it. Hence, when it comes to rest, it is colder, often much colder, than it was before it was heated.

Of course the expansion of the rising air correspondingly increases the vapor capacity, but it is easy to show, both theoretically and experimentally, that this increase of vapor capacity by volume expansion is small in comparison with its simultaneous decrease through the lowering of the temperature, and that convectional expansion, therefore, whether incident to the blowing of wind up and over mountains, or to local heating, is a most effective means of inducing condensation and the formation of clouds.

CONDENSATION NUCLEI

Whenever ordinary air, kept humid by the presence of water, is suddenly expanded in a closed vessel, it instantly becomes filled throughout with a miniature cloud, precisely as occurs on an incomparably larger scale in nature. Subsequent expansions of the same air, each after the settling of all droplets previously formed, induce less and less cloud, and presently none at all. If filtered air—that is, air drawn through several inches of cotton wool, or other substance of similar texture—is used, condensation by moderate expansion is impossible from the first. The admission, however, of a little smoke restores to the exhausted air, and endows the filtered air with, full powers of condensation. There are, therefore, condensation nuclei in the atmosphere—hundreds and often thousands of them per cubic inch—which can be filtered out; and microscopic examination shows that they consist essentially of dust particles. Hence, hygroscopic dust, moisture, and some cooling process are the three essential factors in all natural fog and cloud formation.

It is true that a few substances other than dust, such as the oxides of nitrogen, act as condensation nuclei, but they seem generally to be negligible in quantity. Furthermore, condensation can be obtained in air wholly free from any such nuclei provided it is ionized and forced to at least a fourfold supersaturation, a degree of humidity that probably never occurs in the free air. Indeed, under very great supersaturation, eight or nine fold, condensation occurs even in perfectly clean nonionized air. But this, too, is only a laboratory experiment, and not a process by which clouds are formed in nature.

DISCOVERY OF CONDENSATION NUCLEI

The indispensable rôle played by condensation nuclei in Nature's marvelous drama of the fog and cloud was first discovered in 1875 by the French scientist Coulier. Almost immediately, however, he published a second paper in which, failing properly to interpret certain additional experiments, he practically repudiated his first and correct conclusions. Hence, and because he did not follow up this investigation to an unequivocal result, the whole phenomenon fell back again into the realm of the unknown. Here it remained until 1880, in which meteorologically memorable year the Scottish amateur (one whose work is done for the love of it and not for a living) John Aitken, through a series of experiments, simple, crucial, and ingenious, and with no knowledge of Coulier's work, rediscovered that wonder rôle in all its essentials—rediscovered it and elaborated it with investigation after investigation, until all the world knew of it and marveled.

SKETCH OF JOHN AITKEN

This eminent scientist about whom, because he was the greatest expounder of condensation, the lover of clouds should be and is inquisitive, was born at Falkirk, Scotland, September 18, 1839. His father, Henry Aitken, was the prosperous head of a local but well known legal firm. He was educated at the Falkirk Grammar School, and the University of Glasgow, where he studied engineering and had the good fortune to attend the inspiring lectures of Sir William Thomson (later Lord Kelvin) on Natural Philosophy.

After serving an apprenticeship of five years in marine engineering, two at Dundee and three at Glasgow with Messrs. Napier and Sons, shipbuilders, his health became so impaired that he gave up all idea of following this or any other profession. However, the amateur's urge and the inspiration of Kelvin still were with him and so, being untrammeled by lack of means, he at once became an independent, quiet and patient seeker of physical truths. He even made of his house a workshop and laboratory, with lathe, bench, and other equipment necessary for fine and accurate work in metal, wood, and glass. Many of his

John Aitken

investigations required original pieces of apparatus, and these he not only designed but also constructed. Here he worked quietly and modestly, but with such success that he became a member of the Royal Societies both of Edinburgh and of London, the former awarding him two prizes and the latter a medal.

He communed humbly with Nature, seeking only the truth, and that for truth's sake; would accept no office of honor; and when the end came, as it did on November 14, 1919, left the bulk of his estate to charities in his own home and native town.

Such was the beautiful life of that modest investigator who, despite poor health, solved for us, in addition to many other things, the master riddle of the fog and the cloud.

COUNTING NUCLEI

Aitken not only proved that ordinary cloud and fog droplets are formed about nuclei, but also counted the number of such nuclei per unit volume in the atmosphere at many places and under various special conditions. His apparatus for this purpose was rather elaborate, for exact results, but in principle was as follows: A polished silver plate lightly ruled into small squares, generally one millimeter on the side, is set level in a vessel of considerable size and within half a centimeter, say, of a detached, flat, horizontal cover. This vessel, containing some water, and whose remaining volume is known, is then filled with dust-free air, and into that in turn is admitted a measured volume of the air whose nuclei are to be counted. After the two samples of air, the dusty and the dust-free, have had time to become thoroughly mixed, the whole is expanded a known amount sufficient to form a droplet on every nucleus present. The droplets that settle on the silver plate are then counted over several squares and the average per square noted. If millimeter squares are used, and if the plate and its cover are half a centimeter apart, this average number of droplets per square is the number of nuclei per each 1/200 of a cubic centimeter of the expanded volume of the diluted air. Suppose that before expansion the contents of the vessel are at atmospheric pressure and that the dusty air admitted is 10 per cent of the whole volume. Let the expansion be 20 per cent, and let the average number of droplets per square be one. That is, let each cubic centimeter of the original dusty air occupy, on expansion, 12 cubic centimeters, and let there fall one droplet out of each 1/200 cubic centimeter of this diluted and expanded air. Then each cubic centimeter of the original or undiluted atmosphere contains 200 × 1 × 12, or 2400, condensation nuclei, or 39,329 per cubic inch, a fairly average outdoors number.

ORIGIN AND NATURE OF NUCLEI

The more common varieties of the condensation nuclei in the atmosphere are: (1) Mineral dust, finely divided or disintegrated particles of rock caught up by passing winds; (2) vegetable fibers, largely the remains of decaying leaves and other rubbish, scattered through the air by winds and convection; (3) pollen from many kinds of vegetation, especially trees, such as the maples and conifers, in the spring of the year, and grasses and weeds during the summer and fall; (4) spores, bacteria, and the like, scattered hither and thither by every wind that blows; (5) soot, unburnt carbon particles and mineral ash from furnaces, domestic ranges, forest fires, and all other such sources; (6) salt particles, mainly from evaporated sea spray; these are the chief nuclei over the ocean, and are important even far inland; (7) hygroscopic droplets, if masses so minute may be called droplets, formed by the union of water vapor with such hygroscopic gases as ammonia and the oxides of nitrogen, themselves due, largely at least, to electric discharges, and the oxides of sulphur, produced mainly by the burning of coal; (8) volcanic ash, explosively ejected by many an eruption, occasionally to great heights, and there wafted around the world; (9) meteoric or cosmical dust, the ashes, so to speak, of the daily millions of meteors that burn in our atmosphere.

These are not all the sources of nuclei—of atmospheric dust and pollution—but they are most if not all the principal sources, and enough to prepare us to accept as true the statement that it would take one a month to count the number of such particles he generally inhales with every single breath.

Obviously, when the point of water vapor saturation is passed in the free air, the condensation that produces fog or cloud occurs first on the more hygroscopic particles, the ammoniacal and acid droplets, and especially the motes of sea salt. It is only after these more hygroscopic nuclei have been removed from the atmosphere that the less hygroscopic varieties can become effective. Hence adding non-hygroscopic dust to humid air does not materially alter the density of any fog that may be formed therein, either artificially or naturally.

A detailed account of humidity, evaporation and condensation may be found in PHYSICS OF THE AIR and elsewhere.

Chapter II

FOGS

> I run the scale from finest veil
> That e'er Arachne spun,
> To deepest gloom, impending doom
> As to a soul undone.

DISTINCTION BETWEEN FOG AND CLOUD

As already explained, whenever the air is cooled, by any means whatever, below its dew point, a portion of the water vapor present separates out on such hygroscopic dust particles or other condensation nuclei as happen to be present. If this process occurs only at a considerable distance above the surface of the earth, leaving the lower air clear, the result is some form of cloud. If, on the other hand, it extends quite to, or occurs at, the surface of the earth it is then called a fog, no matter how shallow or how deep it may be. The distinction, therefore, between fog and cloud is that of position. Fog is a cloud on the earth; cloud, a fog in the sky.

In some cases the only basis of distinction between fog and cloud is that of viewpoint. For example, the mist that sometimes covers only the crest of a mountain generally is called fog by those actually in it, and cloud, at the same time, by those in the valley below.

WHERE AND HOW FOGS ARE FORMED

Fogs are likely to form along rivers and large creeks and in the mountain valleys of all but arid regions in the latter part of any still cloudless night of summer or autumn. During these seasons the streams and the humid soil are warm, especially when exposed to sunshine, and hence evaporate much moisture into the lower atmosphere, where, in great measure, it remains when there are no winds to blow it away.

Throughout the night, however, the surface of the soil and the adjacent humid air, by virtue of its humidity, lose heat rapidly by radiation to the colder atmosphere above and to the sky, or empty space, beyond. This loss of heat by radiation is no greater, of course, by night than in the daytime, but when there is no sunshine to make good such loss, or do better—as generally is the case through the forenoon—the inevitable consequence is a lowering of the temperature. Hence, during approximately calm, clear nights the temperature of the humid lower air often falls below the dew point and a fog of corresponding depth and density is formed. If the air were absolutely still, which it seldom is, if ever, fog would not accumulate to any appreciable depth. It would fall out as fast as formed if there were no convectional or turbulent mixing of the surface air.

When the sky is overcast there commonly is enough radiation from the clouds back to the earth, especially when they happen to be low (hence warm), to prevent the cooling of the surface air to the dew point and the consequent formation of fog. Neither does fog form when there is considerable wind, partly because the more humid lower air is then mixed with the drier upper air and the surface dew point thereby lowered, and partly because this mixing prevents much fall in the surface temperature by distributing the loss of heat through a relatively large amount of air instead of leaving it confined essentially to that near the ground. Hence fogs of the kind under consideration—radiation fogs, summer fogs, land fogs, valley fogs—seldom occur either when the sky is cloudy or the night windy.

Another source of numerous fogs is the drifting of relatively warm humid air over places much colder,

22   FOGS, CLOUDS AND AVIATION

Fig. 1. Frost Smoke. Antarctic Shore. Taken on British Antarctic Expedition, 1910–1913

Ponting, photo

such as the drifting of on-shore winds over snow banks. In this way the humid air frequently is cooled below its dew point and fog—"winter fog" or "sea fog"—produced. Likewise, heavy fogs often are formed when the wind is from warm to cold water—from the Gulf Stream to the Labrador Current, for instance.

Fogs also frequently occur when cold air slowly flows in over warm water. This explains the "frost smokes" of polar seas, Fig. 1, and the "steaming" of rivers and lakes on cold frosty mornings. In these cases the relatively warm water goes on evaporating into the cold air even after it becomes saturated and thereby produces a water droplet or a minute ice crystal about every one of the myriad millions of nuclei present. If, however, the cold air comes in with a rush—that is, if it enters as a strong wind—no fog is produced, simply because the vapor is distributed by the accompanying turbulence through too large a volume to produce saturation.

KINDS OF FOG

In respect to the ways in which they are formed, fogs may be divided into two classes:

1. *Radiation fog* (Figs. 2 and 3), due to the cooling

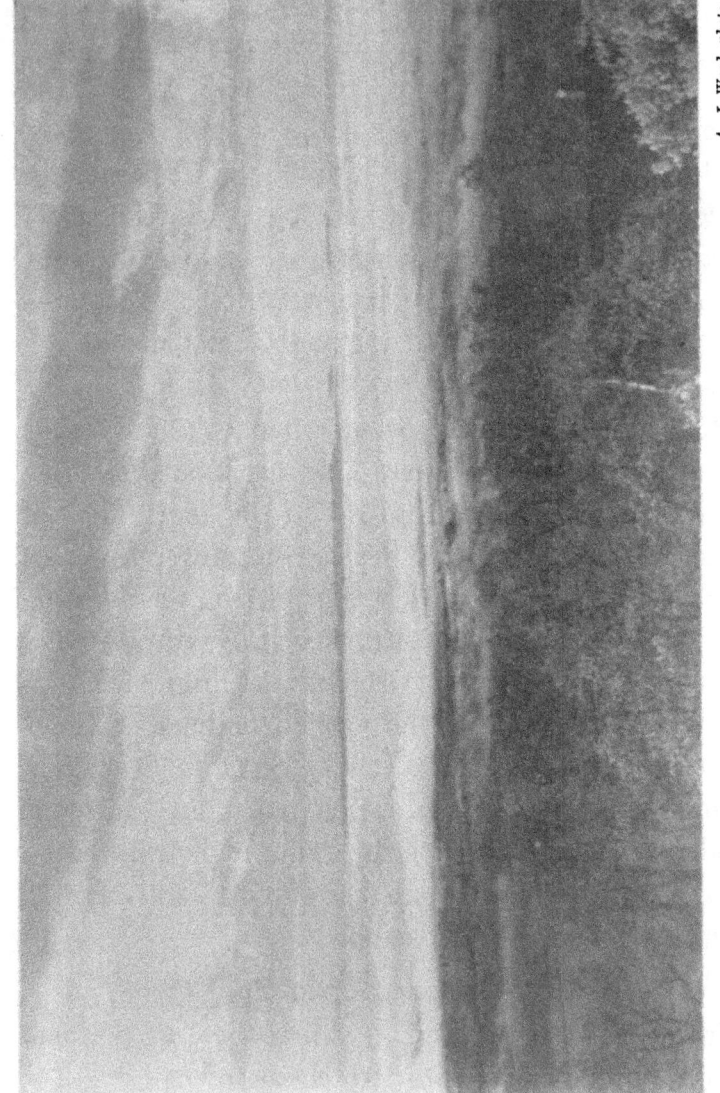

Fig. 2. Radiation Fog. Loudoun Valley, Va.

A. J. Weed, photo

FOGS 25

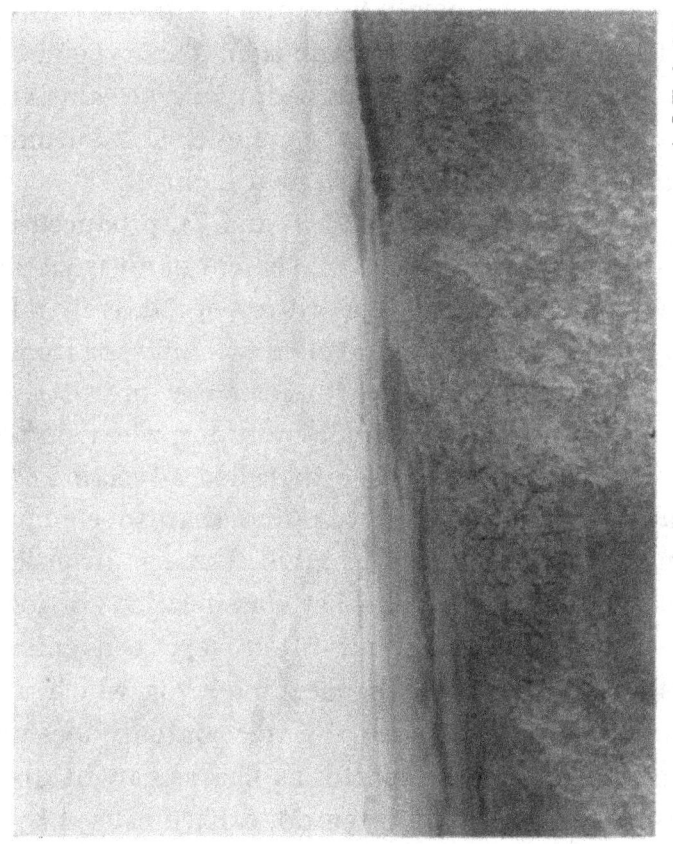

A. J. Weed, photo.

FIG. 3. Radiation Fog. Loudoun Valley, Va.

of the lower air below the dew point, partly by its own radiation and partly by contact with the surface which itself had cooled by radiation. This type of fog is common, as already explained, along streams and in valleys where, through the summer and autumn, it is apt to occur on any calm, clear night.

2. *Advection fog* (Figs. 4, 5, 6 and 7), produced by the advection or horizontal movement of air from one place to another such as the drifting of relatively mild air from the ocean inland over snow banks, or from a warm current to a cold one; and the flow of frosty air over open water. Furthermore, any fog when shifted to a new position may then be called advection fog. Usually, too, the shifted fog, like that so common on many leeward coasts, is advective also in origin.

There also are several other classifications of fogs, less scientific perhaps, but often very convenient. Thus we speak of *dry fog*, meaning a fog which, because of the small amount of water content, does not wet our clothing—evaporates as fast as caught up—or else meaning, as we often do, a haze caused by a forest fire, dust storm, or volcanic explosion; *wet fog*, meaning one containing so much water that, like a Scotch mist, it makes at least the surface of one's

FIG. 4. Advection Fog; Row of Coast Cumuli in Distance. Seen from Mount Wilson, Calif.

F. Ellerman, photo.

Fig. 5. Advection Fog. Seen from Mount Wilson, Calif.

F. Ellerman, photo.

FIG. 6. Advection Fog. Seen from Mount Wilson, Calif.

Fig. 7. Advection Fog. Seen from Mount Wilson, Calif.

F. Ellerman, photo.

clothing distinctly damp; *sea fog*, fog originating on the ocean, whether remaining there or drifting on shore; *land fog*, one occurring in the country and which, as its nuclei are but slightly hygroscopic, quickly evaporates; *city fog*, also called *smog*, a telescoped compound of smoke and fog, one occurring over a city, especially a city that uses a large amount of soft coal and has but few smoke consumers, generally slow to evaporate, owing jointly, presumably, to the hygroscopic nature of the nuclei and to the oil in the unburned sooty smoke; *black fog*, one containing a great amount of soot, such as occasionally forms over large, smoky cities; *pea-soup fog*, a local name given to those London fogs that contain only a moderate amount of smoke particles—just enough to give the fog a distingly yellowish cast; *ice fog*, or "frost smoke," the fog of polar seas, caused by the drifting over them of very cold air; and many others, mostly of less interest and of small importance.

QUANTITY OF WATER IN A FOG

It might seem, on first thought, that it would be a very easy thing to measure the amount of liquid water in a given volume of fog, but this amount is so small that even tolerably accurate measurements of it require much care. Nevertheless, it has been reliably measured. Thus, in the course of an official ice patrol cruise on the *Seneca* about the southern edge of the Grand Banks of Newfoundland, that is, in the region of one of the most frequented of the steamer lanes, Wells and Thuras measured the water content of a dense fog that occurred on the evening of May 9, 1915. The method they used,[1] probably the best yet devised, was as follows: (1) The foggy air was slowly drawn through a fine wire grating sufficiently heated electrically to evaporate all the droplets. (2) The water vapor content per unit volume of this slightly warmed air was determined in the usual way, that is, from the readings in it of adequately ventilated wet and dry bulb thermometers, and the reference of these values to suitable hygrometric tables. (3) From the value thus obtained, corrected to the temperature of the free or untreated air, was subtracted the vapor content per equal volume of the latter, assuming it to be saturated. This difference clearly was the mass of

[1] U. S. Coast Guard. Bulletin No. 5, International Ice Observation and Ice Patrol Service in the North Atlantic Ocean. Gov. Printing Office, Washington, D. C., 1916.

liquid water per given volume of the undisturbed foggy air, always surprisingly small. In their report they say: "To gain some idea of the order of magnitude of the quantities involved in this dense fog, assume that one can not see beyond 100 feet. A block of fog 3 feet wide, 6 feet high and 100 feet long contains less than one-seventh of a glass of liquid water. This water is distributed among 60 billion drops."

Barely one good swallow!

SIZE AND NUMBER OF FOG PARTICLES

The size of fog particles is easily and accurately determined by looking through the fog at a distant point (pinhole) source of bright light, or light otherwise rendered parallel, and noting the difference in direction toward center and circumference of any definite one of the rings of colored light seen around this source—rings of precisely the same nature as the coronae produced by thin clouds around the sun and moon. This angular size, or difference in direction between center and circumference of any one of these rings, increases as the diameter of the fog particles decreases, and in such known and definite manner that when either is given the other can at once be accurately calculated.

If then, we know the size of the fog particle and if, in addition, we know the amount of liquid water in a given volume of fog, which, as explained above, can be measured, it obviously is only a matter of easy arithmetic to find the number of such particles per cubic inch, say, or any other given volume.

These sizes and numbers, however, are surprising. Everyone knows, of course, that a fog droplet is small, but not many, perhaps, realize that 2,500 of them, of the average size, placed side by side in a straight row would extend only one inch, or, in other words, that it would take half an hour to count a string of them an inch long! Nor is the number of fog particles in a definite volume any less amazing. It is but a light fog that has only 1,000 droplets per cubic inch; a heavy fog has around 20,000. Indeed, vastly greater numbers have often been found, even up to nearly a million per cubic inch.

But these droplets, as explained, are so excessively minute that the very maximum density of a million per cubic inch would still leave the empty space

30,000 times greater than the volume actually occupied by all the liquid present.

FOG IMPRESSIONS

If one would thrill his soul with beauty let him, on a brilliant, moonlit night, view from the mountain's crest a far flung fog over all the piedmont region beyond, with foothills and knolls rising here and there as so many enchanted islands in an enchanted sea. Let him, as the dawn breaks clear, gaze from a mountain top on an incipient, fibrous fog, covering a neighboring valley with a fabric more gauzy and delicate than ever Arachne spun. Let him stand on the topmost peak of rugged Tamalpais and watch in wonder the mighty fog billows crowd through the Golden Gate, break over the barrier mountain crests, and rush down their sides in an all engulfing flood. Let him view from afar the snow-crowned crest of incomparable Fuji, floating without visible support, in a clean, clear sky while all its base and the region around is lost in deep fog and delicate mist.

These are but some, and typical, of the most beautiful and fascinating of fog effects; so impressive, indeed, that we could not forget them if we would, and so charming that certainly we would not forget them if we could.

But the impressions produced by fog are not always so charming and entrancing. If one would go quite to the opposite extreme and experience its terrors, let him get lost in London's darkest and densest fog. Let him be alone at night in an unfamiliar forest and have settle down upon him so thick a fog that literally he can not see his hand before him. Let him, on the ocean in the dead of night, between the shrieks of his own ship's siren hear from somewhere, just somewhere, within the encircling gloom, the same dread warning. Let him, when flying over strange territory, be forced to land in a deep, dense fog!

All these, and many others, are horrors that, once experienced, forever make hideous memory.

And so it is that, from extreme to extreme, from fascination to fear, from delights we fondly cherish to dreads we fain would forget, fog in all its moods and circumstances plays compellingly upon the whole gamut of human emotions.

FOGS AND AVIATION

The light fog known as *frost smoke* is of little importance to the aviator except as an aid in locating open water, especially in long leads or cracks in the surface ice.

Radiation or Land Fog, common of clear calm nights and early mornings during summer and autumn along rivers and streams and in mountain valleys generally is of only minor importance to aviators. It is shallow and though an interference to landing normally so restricted in width as to be easily avoided, or gotten away from.

Advection Fog, however, may be anything from just pretty to menacing and dangerous. The drifted land, or radiation, fog and the sea fog that is caused by the blowing of cold air over relatively warm water both belong to the "just pretty" sort, being shallow and usually of rather small extent. But the real-to-goodness advection fog that forms in warm humid air as it drifts across cold water, or onto cool land, is a thing to keep out of except, perhaps, when playing tag with an enemy. It is deep, normally hundreds to thousands of feet and in many cases quite extensive. It is common whenever warm and cold ocean currents, such as the Gulf Stream and the Labrador Current are close together, and everywhere over high latitude seas. Hence a knowledge of the actual direction of the wind and of the surface temperatures round about together furnish better evidence as to where a fog of this kind is, or soon will be, than does any map of fog frequency. Of course a statistical fog map is helpful in route planning, but alone of little worth as a guide to actual or imminent fog conditions.

As implied above, a dense fog of this sort is an ideal place to hide in when the enemy is about to get you, and an equally fine one to sneak out of when either trying to get away or make a surprise return attack—only the fog is not always there when you need it.

Chapter III

CLOUD FORMS

Have you ever, looking up, seen a dark cloud like to a Centaur, a Leopard, a Wolf, or a Bull?—Aristophanes, *Clouds*.

HOW CLOUDS GOT THEIR NAMES

It is passing strange that the ancient Arabs, Greeks, and others should have given a name to every portion of the heavens, and to numerous individual stars—names still in current use throughout the civilized world—and yet have failed to name any one of the many kinds of clouds that are even more conspicuous in the sky than the stars themselves or their constellations. Perhaps giving them names long seemed both useless and impracticable owing to their infinite variety and ceaseless changes, for indeed, as Shakespeare puts it:

> Sometimes we see a cloud that's dragonish,
> A vapour sometimes like a bear or lion,
> A towered citadel, a pendent rock,
> A forked mountain, a blue promontory
> With trees upon't that nod unto the world
> And mock our eyes with air.
> That which is now a horse, even with a thought,
> The rack dislimns and makes it indistinct
> As water is in water.

But whatever the cause, there was not, down the ages, until the very modern year 1801, any attempt whatever to classify the clouds, although from the beginning everybody everywhere talked about the weather and many wrote about it. This first attempt, made in 1801, as just stated, was by the French naturalist, Lamarck. It received little attention, however, and no general acceptance; owing in part, presumably, to the fact that it was expressed in the words and phrases of a distinctly local or national language unfamiliar to the world at large.

But the time for a practical classification of the clouds was ripe. The need for it was felt by the large number of educated and cultured people who were then taking an active and inquisitive interest in the weather and its ways. Hence in a little while another classification was proposed, this time, 1803, by the Englishman, Luke Howard. Like that of Lamarck, it, too, was based on the *appearance* of the clouds, but the names, instead of being only locally understood, were all in tolerably familiar Latin—the Esperanto of the day. At any rate, whether this universal language had much to do with it or not, Howard's classification soon became well known and extensively used; so much so indeed that all subsequent practical classifications have been but extensions of this original one published in 1803, with the addition, perhaps, of a few unusual and, commonly, unimportant types, some of which Howard probably never saw.

Howard did not tell us how clouds are formed. That was done two or three generations later by Aitken, as already explained, but he greatly admired their beauty, and from childhood to old age observed them closely. He must have loved to talk about them too, for while still a young man he did the science of meteorology the inestimable service of so naming and classifying them that people could converse about them understandingly one with another. Furthermore, his classification, though general, had the great merit of being comprehensive. His "cirrus," for example, included all or nearly all clouds of conspicuous structure caused by differential horizontal motion of the air; his "cumulus" those of marked forms due to differential vertical motion; and his "stratus" any cloud, including fog, that is spread out in a formless horizontal sheet.

SKETCH OF LUKE HOWARD

Who then was this godfather to nephology, this christener of the clouds? He was born in London, November 28, 1772, of Quaker parents, and went to a country school in North Oxfordshire where, as he later lamented, he "learnt too much of Latin grammar and too little of anything else." But he did learn, better, perhaps, than he realized, of some other things, for the appeal of Nature was to him so compelling that while yet a child he closely observed the phenomena of the air and noted the forms of the clouds. It seems, too, that, though only eleven years old, he was tremendously impressed by the marvelous sky phenomena of 1783 that followed, and, as we now know, were caused by, the catastrophic explosion of the volcano Asama Yama in Japan.

From school he went to Stockport as apprentice to a chemist. Here, during spare time, he studied French, botany, and chemistry. The works of the great martyr chemist Lavoisier, for instance, he described as "like sunrise after morning moonlight." A few years later he was a chemist (English sense; druggist, or pharmacist, one would say in America) on his own

LUKE HOWARD

account at Plaistow, where he also continued his observations of the sky. During the winter of 1802-3 he read his epochal paper, "On the Modifications of Clouds," in which they first were given the names they still retain, at a meeting of the Askesian Society of London. This was published in Tilloch's Philosophical Magazine in 1803.

For many years after this he published various articles in the Athenaeum, and elsewhere, of meteorological interest. His largest work was on the "Climate of London," first edition (1818-20) in two volumes, second (1833) in three. In 1821 he was elected a Fellow of the Royal Society of London.

But at last great sorrows came, as sorrows will. When about 80 years old, his wife, Mariabella Elliot, also a Quaker, to whom he was married in 1796, passed away. His own health became alarmingly poor; and so, feeble and broken with sorrow, he waited a dozen more years for his own end, which came on March 21, 1864, and when of his seven children only two sons remained to cherish a little while his paternal memory.

But his godchildren, Cirrus, Stratus, Cumulus,

Nimbus, are immortal, and they make immortal the fame of that peaceful lover of Nature, Luke Howard, who first gave them the appropriate names they bear.

UNIFORMITY OF CLOUD REPORTS

To obtain uniformity in the cloud reports of professional meteorologists, and of all others who wished to be clearly understood, the International Meteorological Committee published in 1910, with illustrations, substantially the following definitions and descriptions of cloud forms.

In 1922 another International Cloud Commission began a further revision of cloud names and classifications, and published an abridged edition of its conclusions in 1930. These definitions and names differ but little from those given by the earlier Commission. However they now are used by all meteorological services, and therefore their more concise portions are here quoted in italics. The enclosed letters next after each type name are its customary abbreviation.

This latest classification of the clouds, a modification and extension of Howard's, is also, like it, based on mere *appearance* and not on any thing really fundamental, such as cause or mode of formation. But however superficial such a classification may be, it nevertheless is the best, perhaps, that can be made, and altogether the most practical. For instance, the mode of origin is not a practical basis for cloud classification, however desirable, because several types of cloud are formed in different ways and frequently one can not be certain just what the actual way really was.

The supplementary remarks, after each of the following quoted definitions and descriptions, while intrusive in position, may, it is hoped, be of some service to those who are not yet cloud experts.

INTERNATIONAL DEFINITIONS AND DESCRIPTIONS OF CLOUD FORMS, AND SUPPLEMENTARY REMARKS

1. *Cirrus (Ci.).—Detached clouds of delicate and fibrous appearance, without shading, generally white in color, often of a silky appearance.*

"Cirrus clouds take the most varied shapes, such as isolated tufts of hair, *i.e.*, thin filaments on a blue sky, branched filaments in feathery form, straight or curved filaments ending in tufts (called *cirrus uncinus*), and others. Occasionally cirrus clouds are arranged in bands, which traverse part of the sky as arcs of great circles, and as an effect of perspective appear to converge at a point on the horizon and at the opposite point also, if they are sufficiently extended. Cirro stratus and cirro cumulus also are sometimes similarly arranged in long bands." (Figs. 8, 9, 10, 11, 12, 13, 14, 15, 16, 17, 18, 19 and 20.)

An interesting form of cirrus clouds is the familiar "mares' tails" (Figs. 14, 15, 16), especially when a considerable number of them occur in the same region of the sky. These are only thin streaks of fine snow crystals into which a little ball of rising cloud is drawn out, partly by the slow descent of the snow itself, and partly by the change, usually an increase, of wind velocity with elevation.

The cirrus occurs up to (and usually at) greater heights than any other type of cloud—roughly 5 miles in polar regions, 7 in middle latitudes, and 9 within the Tropics. Since it occurs above all other clouds it also is the coldest, ranging, roughly, from 50°F. below zero near the Poles to 90° below in the neighborhood of the Equator, the difference in temperature being due to the difference in height. Fur-

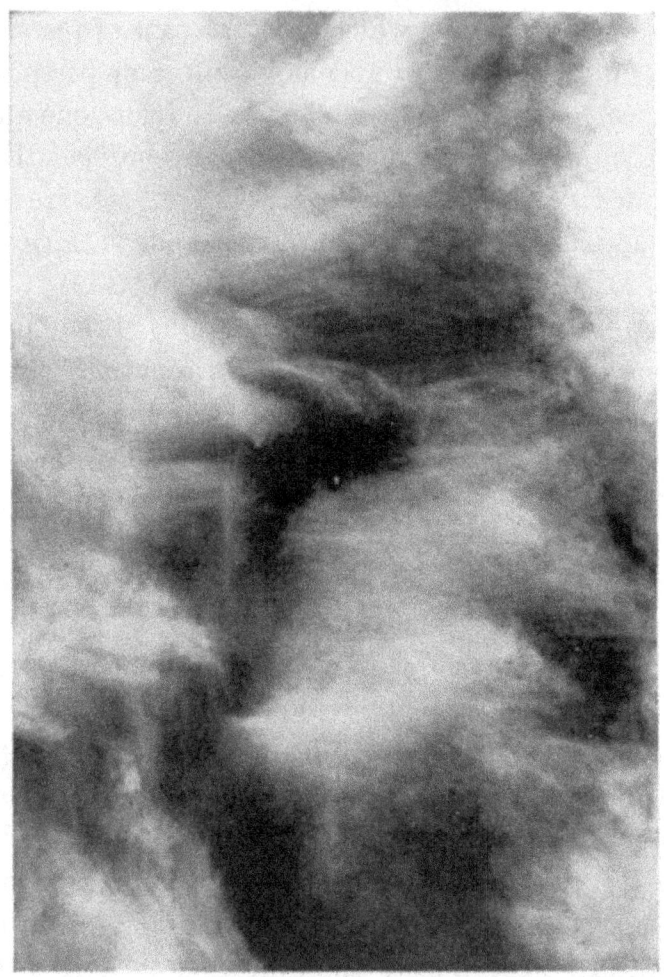

F. *Ellerman, photo.*

FIG. 8. aa. Cirrus (filosus). Seen at Mount Wilson, Calif.

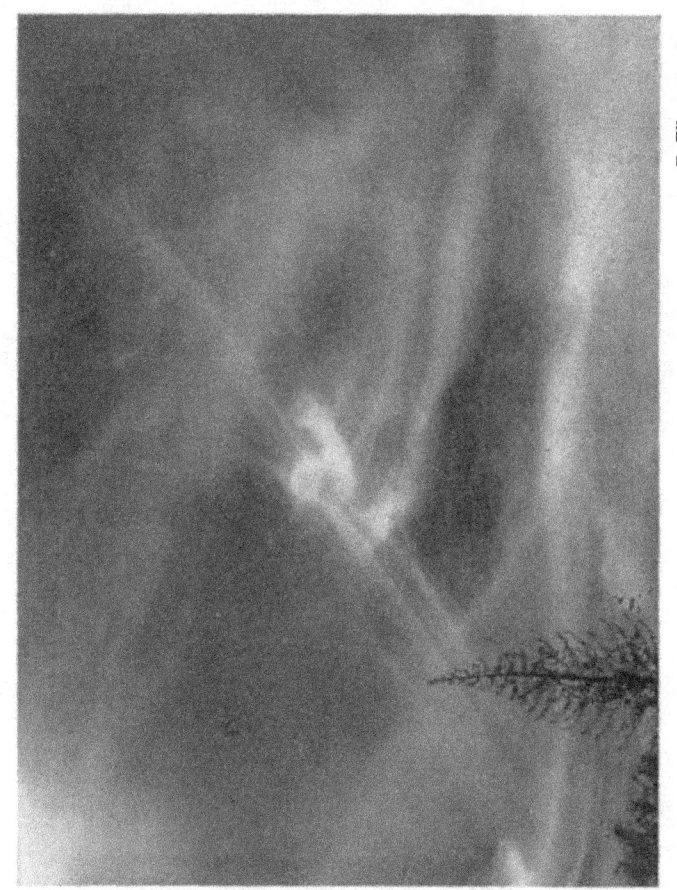

FIG. 9. aa. Cirrus (filosus). Seen at Mount Wilson, Calif.

F. Ellerman photo.

Fig. 10. ab. Cirrus (implexus). Washington, D. C.

FIG. 11. ac. Cirrus (tufted). Washington, D. C.

W. J. Humphreys, photo.

52 FOGS, CLOUDS AND AVIATION

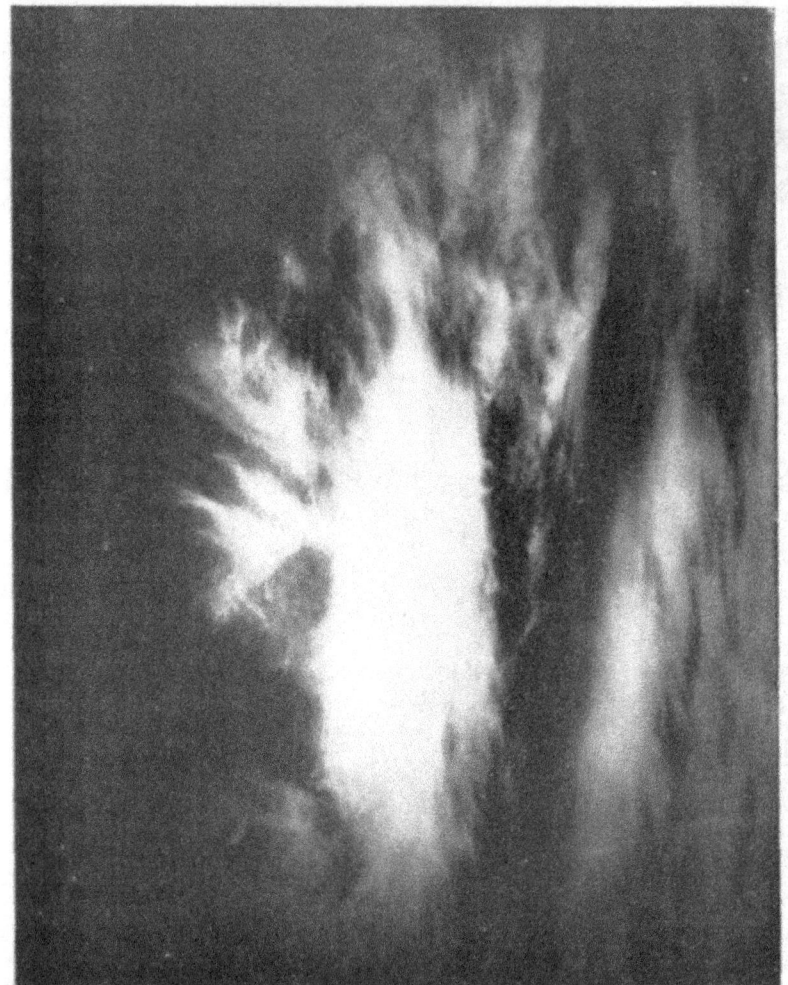

Fig. 12. ac. Cirrus (tufted). Washington, D. C.

W. J. Humphreys, photo.

CLOUD FORMS

F. Ellerman, photo.

FIG. 13. ad. Cirrus (tracto). Seen at Mount Wilson, Calif.

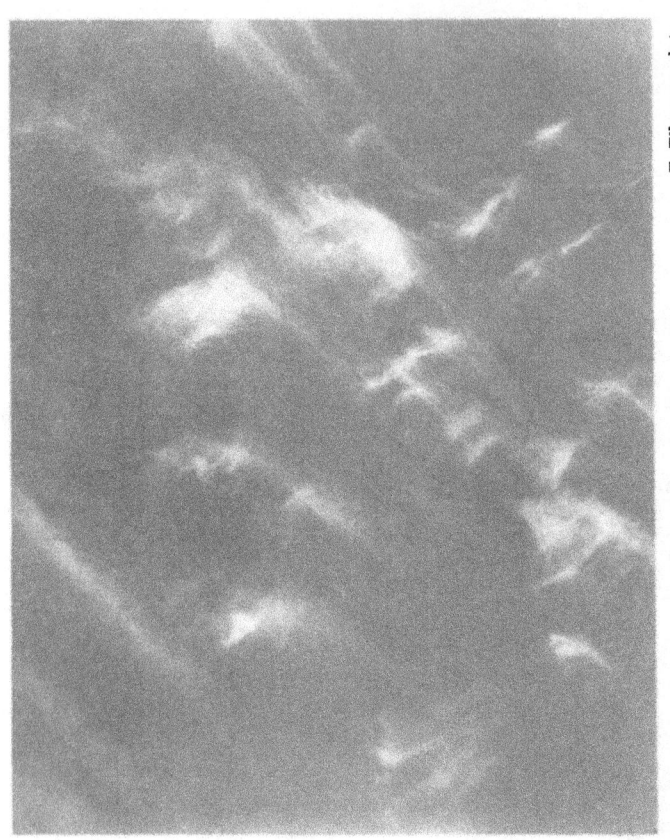

FIG. 14. ae. Cirrus (uncinus or caudatus, Mares' Tails). Seen at Mount Wilson, Calif.

F. Ellerman, photo.

CLOUD FORMS 55

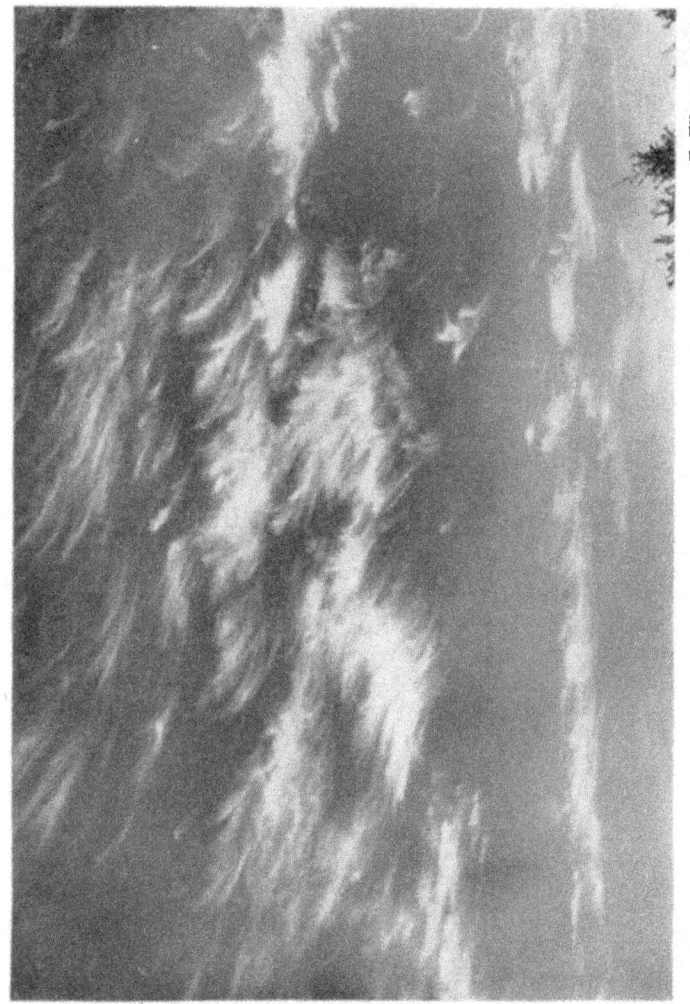

FIG. 15. ae. Cirrus (uncinus or caudatus). Seen at Mount Wilson, Calif.

F. Ellerman, photo.

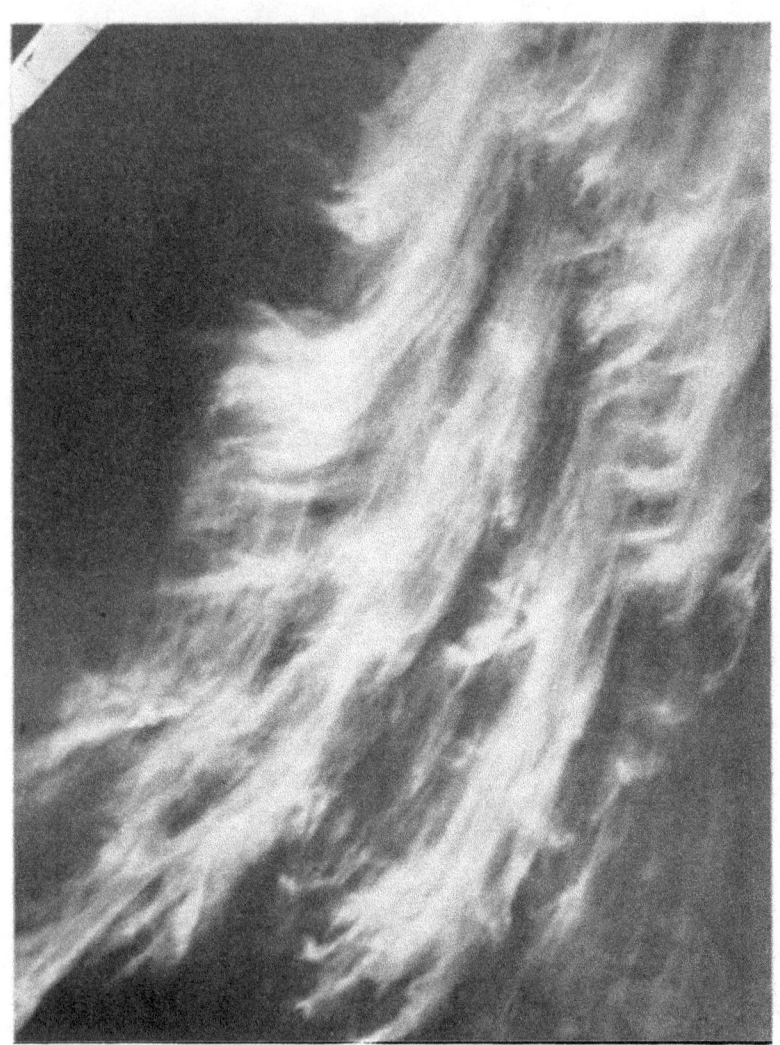

Fig. 16. ae. Cirrus (uncinus or caudatus). Seen at Mount Wilson, Calif.

F. Ellerman, photo.

CLOUD FORMS 57

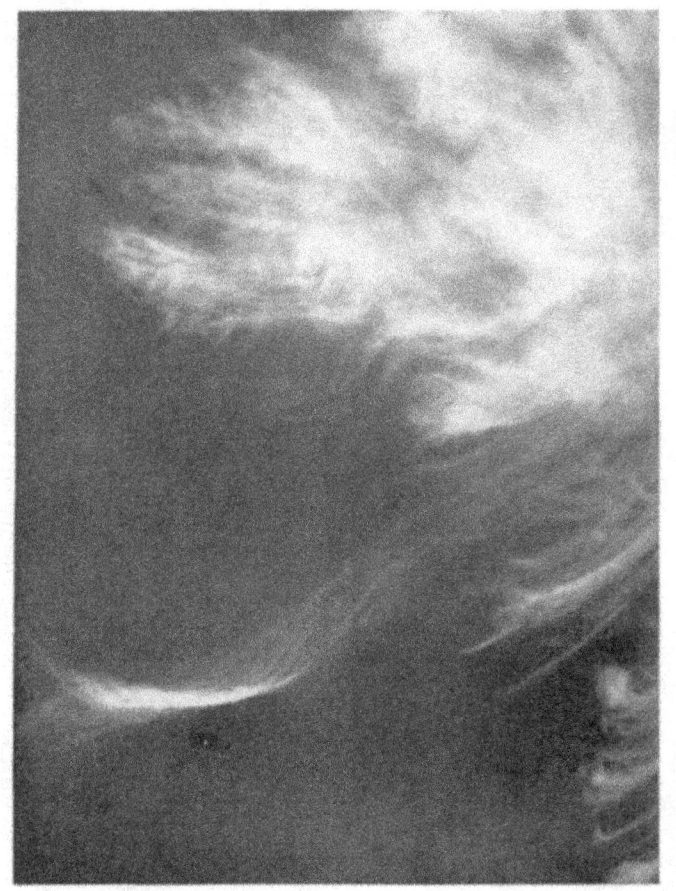

Fig. 17. af. Cirrus (plumeus). Seen at Mount Wilson, Calif.

F. Ellerman, photo.

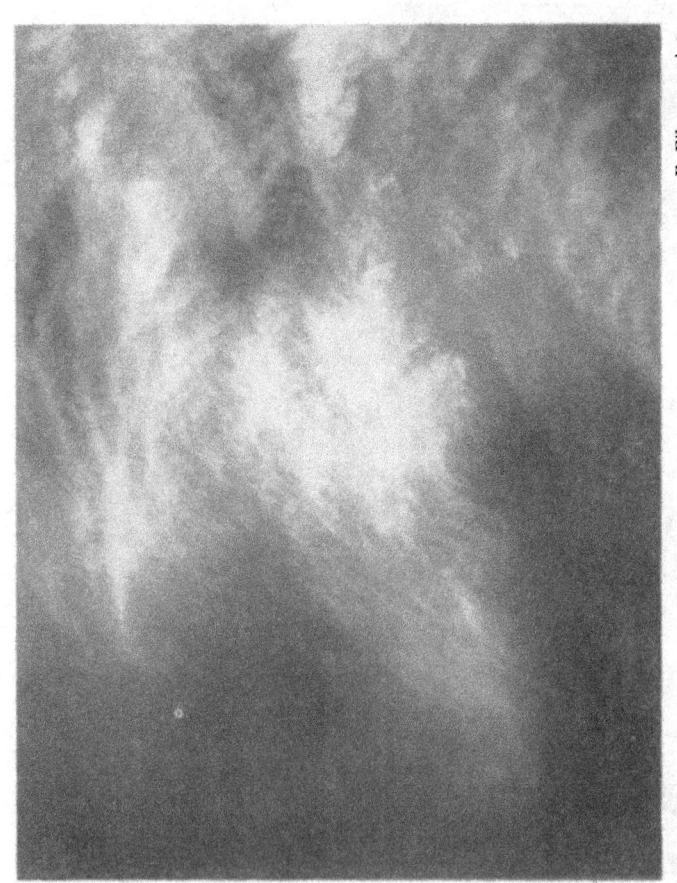

FIG. 18. ag. Cirrus (inconstans), Merging into Cirrocumulus. Seen at Mount Wilson, Calif.

F. Ellerman, photo.

CLOUD FORMS

F. Ellerman, photo.

FIG. 19. ag. Cirrus (inconstans), Merging into Cirrocumulus. Seen at Mount Wilson, Calif.

60 FOGS, CLOUDS AND AVIATION

Fig. 20. a.h. Cirrus (banded, Noah's Ark)

thermore, because it is the coldest of the clouds it likewise is the thinnest, being formed in air whose water content, owing to its low temperature, is very small. Indeed, the sun and moon are sharply outlined through it. Finally, as its temperature is so very low the cirrus nearly always (there seem to be occasional exceptions) consists of snow crystals.

As just stated, the cirrus occurs at higher levels than does any other type of cloud. But it also occurs, under favorable conditions, at any other level, even down to the surface. It is only a shallow, or thin, cloud of tiny snow crystals (except rarely) drawn out by the wind into more or less parallel, fine streaks. Its chief cause appears to be the further cooling, by expansion due to ascent, of air already cold and holding but little moisture, and the dragging out of the slight cloud thus formed into streaks and whirls by the winds in which it occurs.

When the cirrus slowly disappears, leaving a clear sky, fair weather is probable for at least a day or two. On the other hand, when it gradually thickens and merges into a nearly continuous and formless sheet, rain or snow usually begins within a few hours.

To the aviator Cirrus is a valuable one-way screen through which he can look down fairly well, and at the same time be practically hidden from those below.

2. *Cirrostratus (Cist.).*—*A thin, whitish veil, which does not blur the outlines of the sun or moon, but gives rise to halos. Sometimes it is quite diffuse and merely gives the sky a milky look; sometimes it more or less distinctly shows a fibrous structure with disordered filaments.*

The halos here referred to are of two kinds: (*a*) Those due to the refraction of light into rainbow colors on its passage through ice crystals; and (*b*) those produced by the mere reflection of light (hence white or colorless) by the faces of these crystals.

The most common of the first class of halos are: (1) The circle of 22° radius about the sun or moon (Fig. 92); (2) the similar circle of 46° radius; and (3) the circumzenithal arc, a brilliantly colored arc having the point directly overhead as its center, but appearing on the side next the sun only. The chief halos of the second or reflection class are (1) the parhelic circle, a white band of light passing around the sky parallel to the horizon and through the sun

(Fig. 92); and (2) the sun pillar, a vertical column of white light extending directly above and below the sun.

These halos are positive proof that the cirrostratus clouds, like the cirrus from which they frequently are developed, also consist, normally, of myriads of ice crystals.

Whenever the cirrostratus cloud (Fig. 22) has developed from a cirrus it may be assumed that rain or snow, as determined by the temperature, probably will soon follow, not out of the cirrostratus, of course, but from an approaching nimbostratus, or rain cloud.

Though denser than the cirrus, the cirrostratus still is so thin as to leave the outline of the sun sharply defined.

For the aviator the cirrostratus is an even better one-way screen than the cirrus.

3. Cirrocumulus (Cicu.).—A cirriform layer, or patch composed of small white flakes or of very small globular masses, without shadows, which are arranged in groups or lines, or more often in ripples resembling those of the sand on the seashore.

FIG. 21. ba. Cirrostratus, above; Fog below. Seen from Mount Wilson, Calif.

CLOUD FORMS

F. Ellerman, photo.

Fig. 22. ba. Cirrostratus, above; Fog below. Seen from Mount Wilson, Calif.

M. Mott-Smith, photo.

FIG. 23. bb. Cirrostratus, above, Veiling Sun; Cumulus, below

CLOUD FORMS

F. Ellerman, photo.

Fig. 24. ca. Cirrocumulus, Upper and Middle; Cirrus (Mares' Tails) below. Seen at Mount Wilson, Calif.

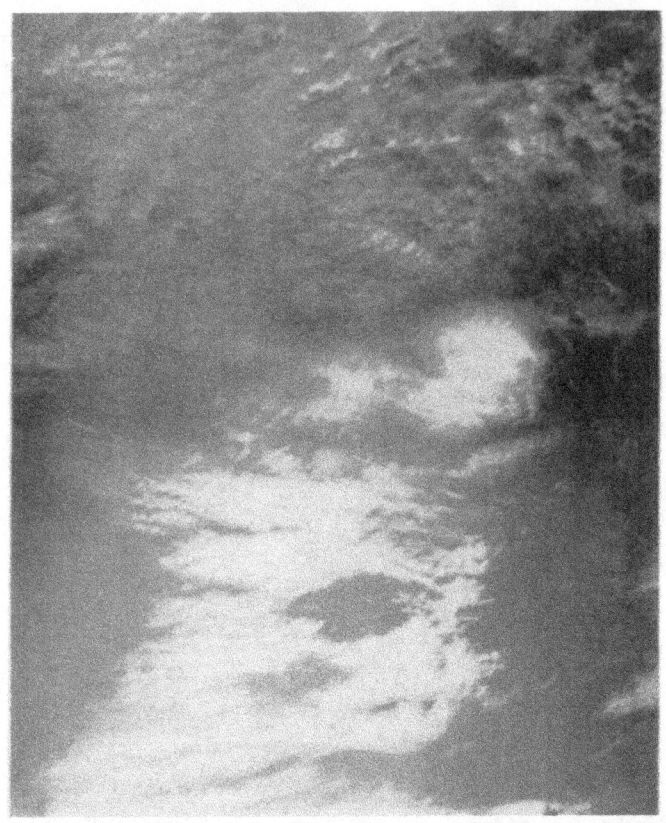

F. *Ellerman, photo.*

Fig. 25. ca. Cirrocumulus. Seen at Mount Wilson, Calif.

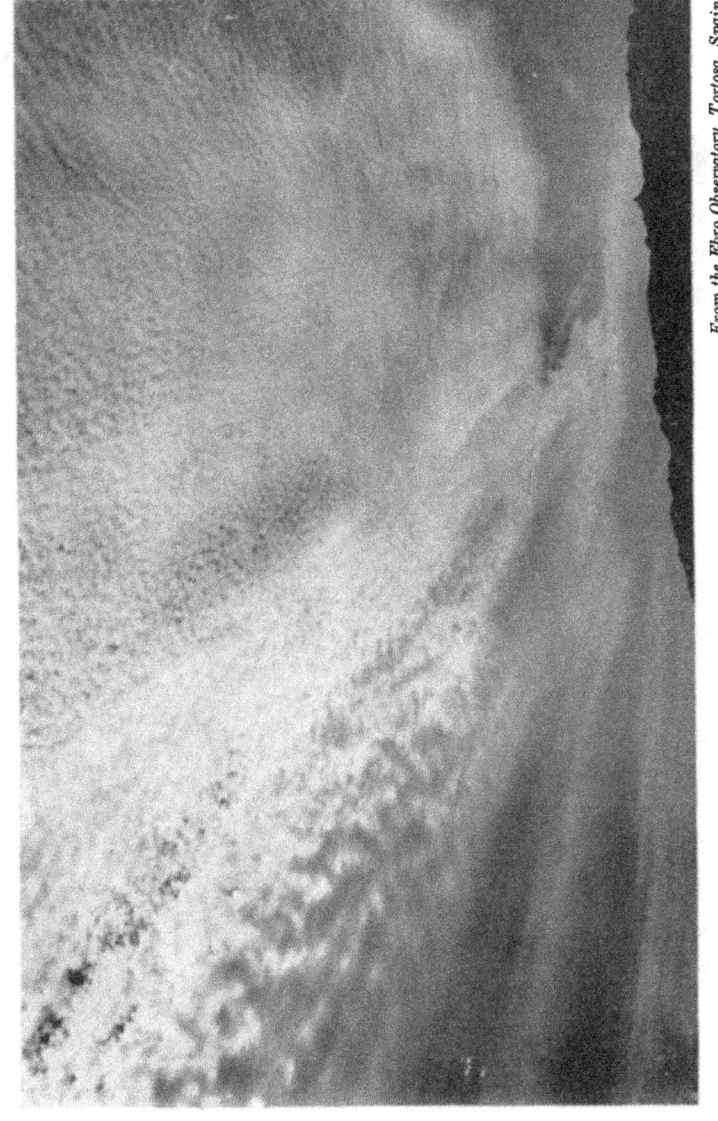

FIG. 26. cb. Cirrocumulus, right; Alto-cumulus, upper left; Alto-stratus, lower left

From the Ebro Observatory, Tortosa, Spain.

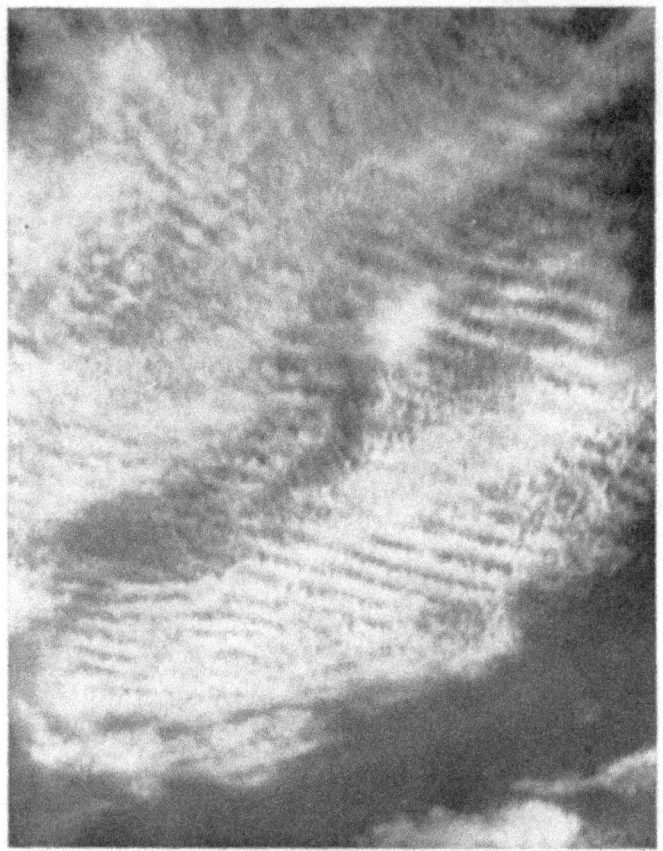

E. E. Barnard, photo.

Fig. 27. cc. Cirrocumulus

This type of cloud is often called "mackerel sky", an abbreviation of "mackerel-back sky," so named because of the frequent resemblance of rows of cirrocumuli to the patterns (not the scales) on the backs of one or more species of mackerel. When the cirrocumuli are small, numerous, and without order or pattern, they often are called "curdled sky." (Fig. 26)

All forms of the cirrocumulus appear to be due to small local convections. Those occurring in rows presumably are on the crests of air waves or billows at the interface between wind layers of unequal speeds or different directions, or both, and commonly unequal also in temperature and humidity. The cirrocumulus, through turbulence or other cause, often merges into a more or less uniform, stratified cloud, especially the cirrostratus.

The fact that the cirrocumuli cast but faint shadows, if any, and that the sharp outline of the sun is visible through them shows that they are quite thin and contain but little cloud material.

The cirrocumulus also is an excellent one-way screen for the aviator.

4. Altocumulus (Acu.).—A layer (or patches) composed of laminae or rather flattened globular masses, the smallest elements of the regularly arranged layer being fairly small and thin, with or without shading. These elements are arranged in groups, in lines, or waves, following one or two directions, and are sometimes so close together that their edges join. The thin and translucent edges of the elements often show irisations, which are rather characteristic of this class of cloud.

"The separate masses are generally larger and more compact (resembling stratocumulus) in the middle region of the group, but the denseness of the layer varies and sometimes is so attenuated that the individual masses assume the appearance of sheets or thin flakes of considerable extent with hardly any shading. At the margin of the group they form smaller cloudlets resembling those of cirrocumulus. The cloudlets often group themselves in parallel lines, arranged in one or more directions." (Figs. 28, 29, 30, 30-a and 31).

Altocumuli obviously are caused by local convections in a layer of nearly saturated air. They frequently form in the early forenoon after a clear sunrise in consequence of scattered convection in a humid layer of air—humid from the evaporation in it of a previous sheet of altocumuli, or owing to moisture

FIG. 28. da. Altocumulus, Undulated (Mackerel Scales). Washington, D. C.

A. J. Henry, photo.

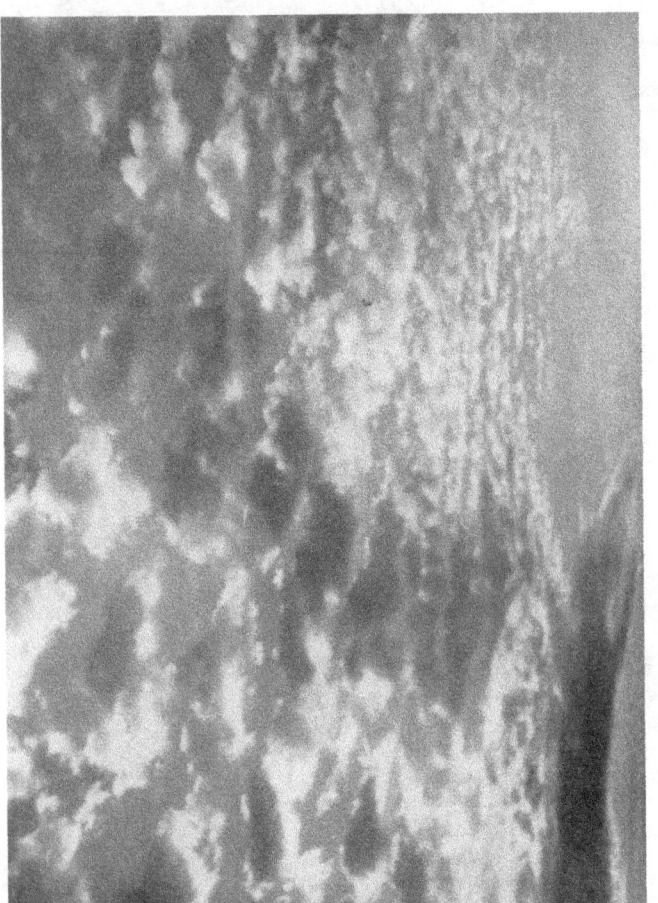

Fig. 29. db. Altocumulus

CLOUD FORMS

FIG. 30. db. Altocumulus

W. J. Humphreys, photo.

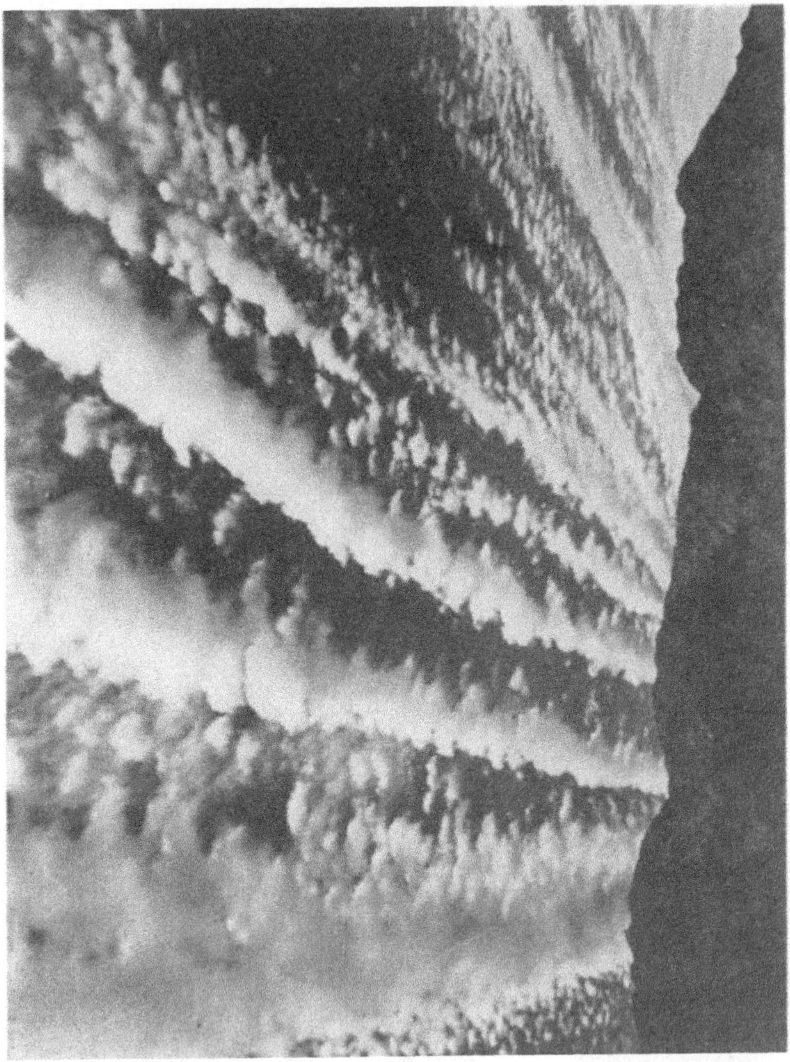

76   FOGS, CLOUDS AND AVIATION

CLOUD FORMS

F. Ellerman, photo.

FIG. 31. dc. Altocumulus (castellatus) above; Cumulus below. Seen from Mount Wilson, Calif.

from the spreadout tops of thunderstorm clouds. After sundown this type of cloud frequently evaporates, paradoxically as a result of getting colder, a condition that favors further condensation. The unexpected consequence, the evaporation instead of condensation, is produced in this way: The cloud particles cool, first by radiation and later both by radiation and evaporation. In turn they cool the air in which they float, which therefore contracts, becomes denser, and sinks, taking the cloud with it. But as it sinks it warms by compression until in the end it comes into equilibrium at some lower level and higher temperature. That is, the cooling of the droplets causes the air that carries them eventually to become warmer and dryer than it was before they first cooled. Hence they evaporate and the cloud they made disappears.

This also is the justification, or explanation, of the old French proverb to the effect that "the moon eats clouds." Of course in this sense the stars do the same thing, but the moon alone gets the credit because night clouds and their changes are well seen only when it is shining.

Occasionally an altocumulus here and there grows to an unwonted height and becomes what is known as an altocumulus castellatus (Fig. 31), a harbinger, as a rule, of coming rain.

Altocumuli are helpful to the aviator when gunning for the other fellow, and especially so when the other fellow is gunning for him. They also, like the cirrocumuli make a tolerably good one-way screen. When above a sheet of altocumuli the aviator still can see very well objects on the earth below, while the anti-aircraft gunner often can not follow him.

5. *Altostratus (Ast.).—Striated or fibrous veil, more or less gray or bluish in color. This cloud is like thick cirrostratus but without halo phenomena; the sun or moon shows vaguely, with a faint gleam, as though ground glass. Sometimes the sheet is thin, with forms intermediate with cirrostratus. Sometimes it is very thick and dark, sometimes even completely hiding the sun or moon. In this case differences of thickness may cause relatively light patches between very dark parts; but the surface never shows relief, and the striated or fibrous structure is always seen in places in the body of the cloud.*

"At other times the sheet is thin like the denser forms of cirrostratus, and through it the sun and the moon may be seen dimly gleaming as through ground glass. This form exhibits all stages of transition between altostratus and cirrostratus, but according to the measurements its normal altitude is about one-half of that of cirrostratus." (Figs. 26 and 32.)

This type of cloud may be formed by the flow of warmer moist air over colder air beneath, by winds dragging out the tops of thunderstorm clouds, or by the cooling in place of a layer of humid air.

The sun and moon when seen through the altostratus, altocumulus, or any other thin cloud of *water droplets*, are surrounded by one or more sets of rings of colored light commonly only two or three diameters of the sun, or moon, away (Fig. 93).

These small circles, in which the red is farthest from the sun or moon are called coronae, and are produced, as just stated, by the action (diffraction) of small water droplets on the light. The much larger circles, called halos, and whose red portions are nearest the sun, or moon, are caused, as previously explained, by the passage of light through *ice crystals*.

The altostratus cloud, being moderately thin, extensive, rather high and nearly opaque, is an ideal screen for the aviator to duck down through to get a view of things below, or to dart up through to get out of sight of enemies on the ground, or through which he can thread up and down in playing hide and seek with opposing planes.

6. *Stratocumulus (Stcu.).—A layer (or patches) composed of globular masses or rolls; the smallest of the regularly arranged elements are fairly large; they are soft and gray, with darker parts.*

"Generally stratocumulus presents the appearance of a gray layer broken up into irregular masses and having on the margin smaller masses grouped in flocks like altocumulus. Sometimes this cloud-form has the characteristic appearance of great rolls of cloud arranged in parallel lines close together. (*Roll cumulus* in England, *Wulst-cumulus* in Germany.) The rolls themselves are dense and dark, but in the intervening spaces the cloud is much lighter and blue sky may sometimes be seen through them. Stratocumulus may be distinguished from nimbostratus by its lumpy or rolling appearance, and by the fact that it does not generally tend to bring rain." (Figs. 33, 34 and 35.)

This cloud, of which there are several forms ranging from the stratus of uneven density (Fig. 34), typical of the rear side of a general storm, through the great parallel rolls to the sheet of well-nigh discrete cumuli, is always due to vertical convection. The more nearly discrete or separate masses are produced by the rising of warm air (thermal convection), while the irregularities in the stratus form appear to be caused, in large part at least, by mechanical turbulence. This last type (Fig. 35) might well be called turbulocumulus. The shallow depth and broad expanse of the stratocumulus often is due to an overlying layer of air of such temperature that the rising, cloud-laden column can not pass through it and hence is forced to spread out, much as rising smoke in a room spreads out under the ceiling.

The stratocumulus offers a fine opportunity for sudden dodging and quick surprises by the expert aviator. It also commonly is turbulent and bumpy.

7. *Nimbostratus (Nbst.).—A low, amorphous, and rainy layer, of a dark gray color and nearly uniform; feebly illuminated, seemingly from inside. When it gives precipitation it is in the form of continuous rain or snow.*

CLOUD FORMS

F. Ellerman, photo.

FIG. 32. ca. Altostratus, above; Fog below. Seen from Mount Wilson, Calif.

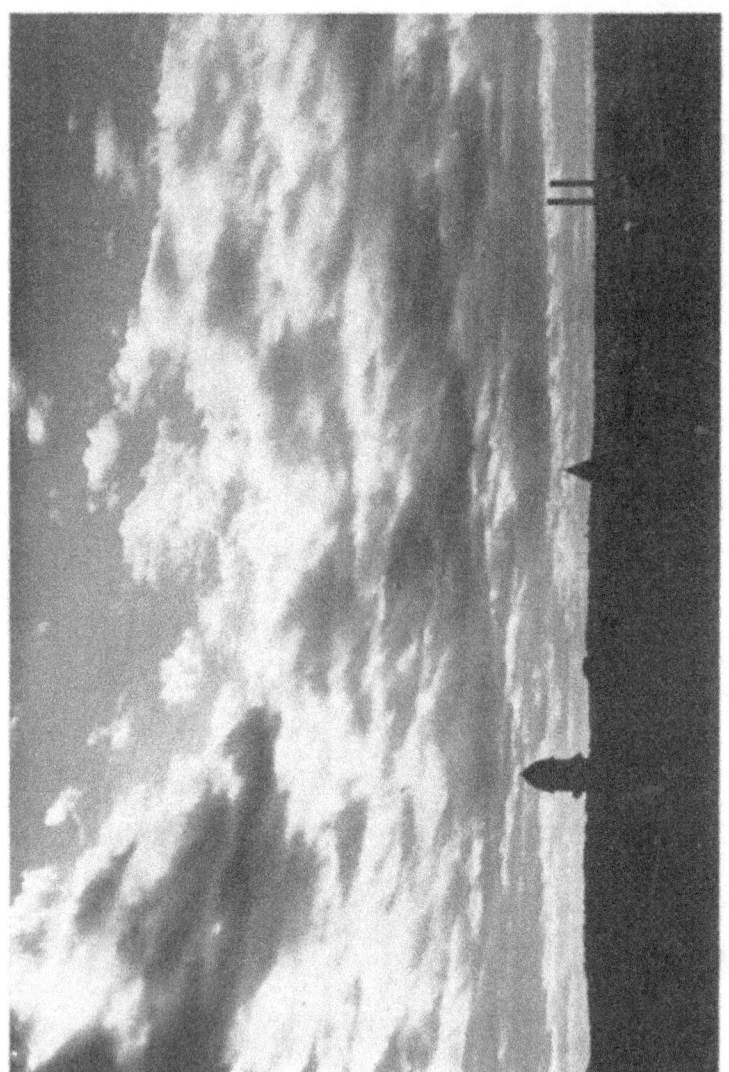

Fig. 33. fa. Stratocumulus. Washington, D. C.

CLOUD FORMS 85

FIG. 34. fb. Stratocumulus. Washington, D. C.

W. J. Humphreys, photo.

86 FOGS, CLOUDS AND AVIATION

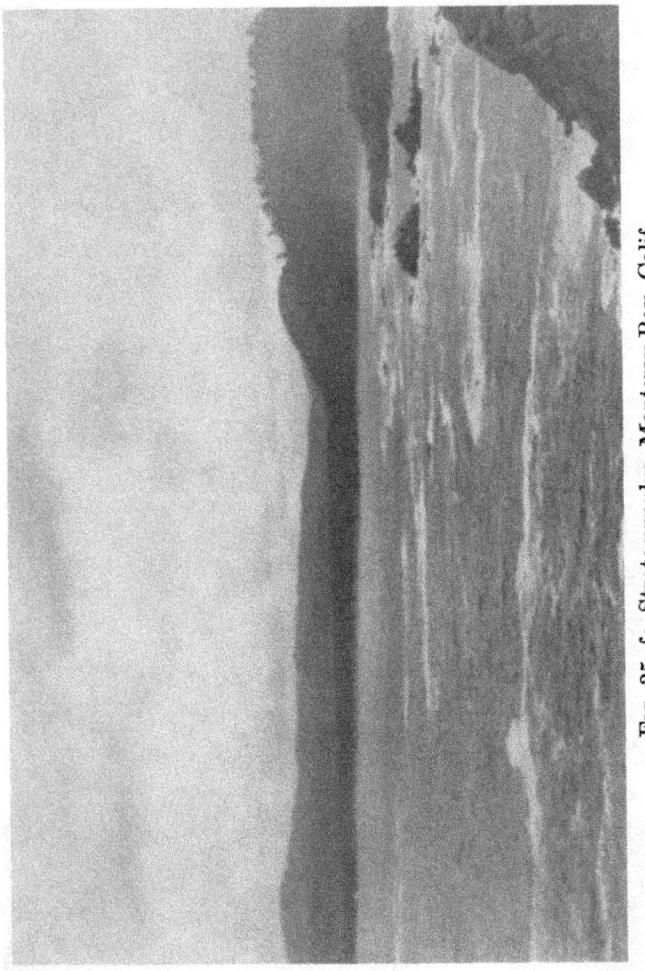

Fig. 35. fc. Stratocumulus. Monterey Bay, Calif.

CLOUD FORMS 87

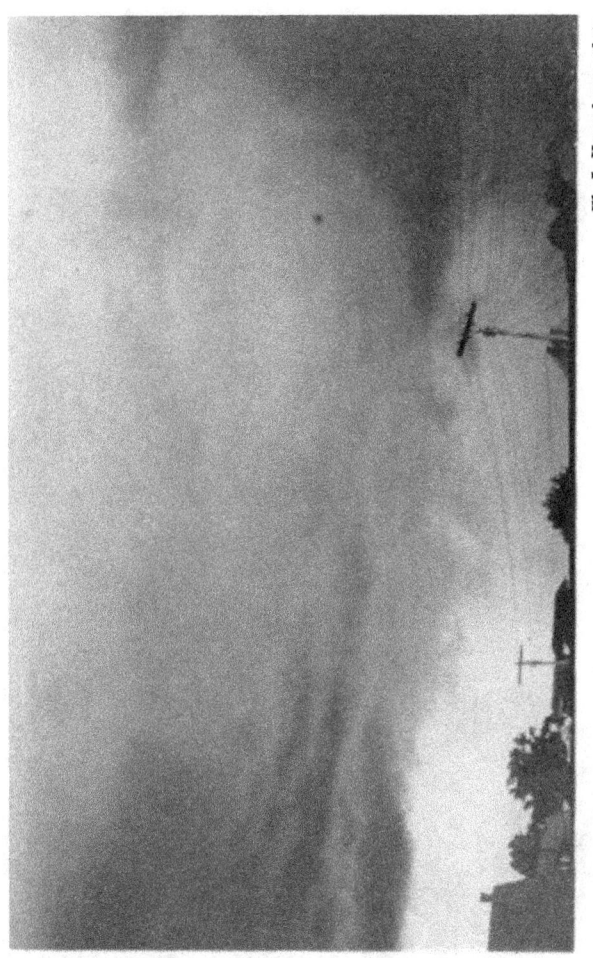

W. J. Humphreys, photo.

FIG. 36. 9a. Nimbus. Ashland, Ky.

Fig. 37. gb. Nimbus, above; Fog below. Seen from Mount Wilson, Calif.

F. Ellerman, photo.

The name of this cloud has evoked much discussion. Its former name, nimbus, originally meaning cloud and, inferentially, storm, and by Howard restricted, apparently, to the "cumulonimbus," described below, now means, in general, any snow or rain cloud except the cumulonimbus. Hence, many argue that if rain or snow is falling from a cloud it certainly is a rain cloud. Likewise, if rain is not falling from it, then clearly it must be some other sort of cloud. But, on the other hand, if a given cloud while raining happens to be a typical rain cloud (nimbostratus), what was it immediately before we saw the rain? Again, if it happens to be raining very hard what shall we call the cloud that we can not see for the rain?

These are typical of the questions and quibbles the arbitrary official definition of "nimbus" has evoked.

As a matter of fact a trace at least, and often more, of precipitation may be falling from a typical altostratus, altocumulus, or other form, which it would be but confusion to call nimbostratus. Similarly, a typical nimbostratus from which rain is falling steadily looks but little different from what it did immediately before the rain began. Hence it is convenient to interpret the definition broadly enough to cover both cases. If the cloud is typically altocumulus, call it altocumulus, whatever may be falling. On the other hand, if it looks like a rain cloud and is not a cumulonimbus, call it nimbostratus, whether it is raining or not.

Of course in taking weather notes it commonly is superfluous to say both rain and nimbostratus cloud, because the former nearly always implies the latter, except in the case of the thunderstorm, which is separately reported. However, if one were noting clouds alone he certainly would find it more convenient, and generally the only thing practicable, to say nimbostratus, or occasionally, nimbus cumuliformis, whenever there is precipitation of considerable intensity without lightning or thunder. The term "altonimbus" might also be useful if only one could be sure that the facts justified it.

This type of cloud is most frequently formed by some kind of mechanical convection, such as ascent due to converging winds, the flow of air over mountain barriers, and the over and under running of currents of different temperatures.

The fractonimbus, or scud, is only a low, ragged

detached fragment of cloud that often rises, like steam, immediately after rainfall on a warm surface, especially the sides of mountains, which it ascends like drifting fog. (Fig. 61.). It also frequently is dragged out of a crest cloud (which see below), by the swirls of the passing wind and hurled down the leeward mountain slope.

The aviator can of course dodge in and out of a nimbostratus from above, but not with safety from below since it often comes down to a low elevation and always is accompanied with poor visibility. When in this cloud one should, if possible, keep away from the level of freezing to a few degrees below freezing, to avoid icing.

8. Cumulus (Cu.).—Thick clouds with vertical development; the upper surface is dome shaped and exhibited rounded protuberances, while the base is nearly horizontal.

"These clouds appear to be formed by ascensional movement of air in the daytime which is almost always observable. When the cloud and the sun are on opposite sides of the observer, the surfaces facing the observer are more brilliant than the margins of the protuberances. When, on the contrary, it is on the same side of the observer as the sun it appears dark with bright edges. When the light falls sideways, as is usually the case, cumulus clouds show deep shadows." (Figs. 38, 39, 40, 41, 42, 43, 44, 45, 46, 47 and 48.)

"True cumulus has well-defined upper and lower margins; but one may sometimes see ragged clouds—like cumulus torn by strong wind—of which the detached portions are continually changing; to this form of cloud the name *fracto cumulus* may be given." (Figs. 49, 50 and 51.)

Even the most casual observation shows the cauliflower heads and sides of cumuli to be in a state of rapid change and constant turmoil. All clouds of this type are caused by the lower air being so much warmer than the upper that it is forced to ascend much as warm air is pushed up a chimney by the heavier cold air on the outside. Hence, even forest fires sometimes cause the formation of cumuli. (Figs. 52 and 52.) However, we should remember that the fire itself adds a surprisingly large amount of moisture to the air—a gallon of water, roughly, for

Fig. 38. Cumulus, Just Building from Fog. Seen from Mount Wilson, Calif.

94 FOGS, CLOUDS AND AVIATION

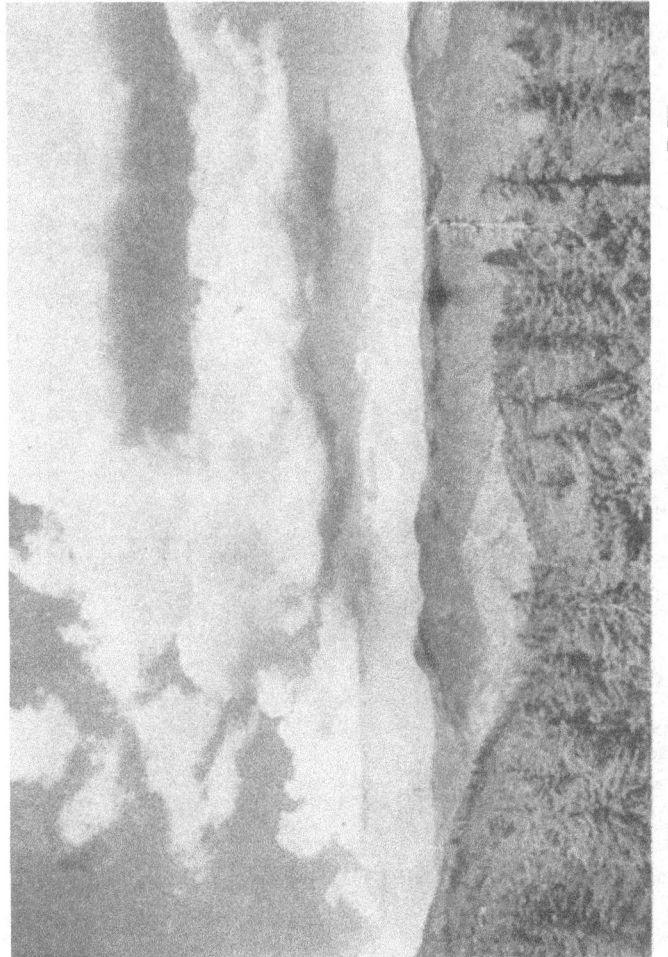

F. Ellerman, photo.

Fig. 39. ha. Cumulus. Seen from Mount Wilson, Calif.

FIG. 40. ha. Cumulus. Monroe County, W. Va. Peters Mountain to left

L. W. Humphreys, photo.

96 FOGS, CLOUDS AND AVIATION

FIG. 41. ha. Cumulus. Grounds, Department of Agriculture, Washington, D. C.

W. J. Humphreys, photo.

CLOUD FORMS

E. B. Calvert, photo.

FIG. 42. hb. Cumulus (en Echelon). Over Loudoun Valley, Va.

98 FOGS, CLOUDS AND AVIATION

F. Ellerman, photo.

FIG. 43. hc. Cumulus, Massive, Seen from Mount Wilson, Calif.

FIG. 44. hc. Cumulus, Massive. Yosemite National Park, Calif.

100 FOGS, CLOUDS AND AVIATION

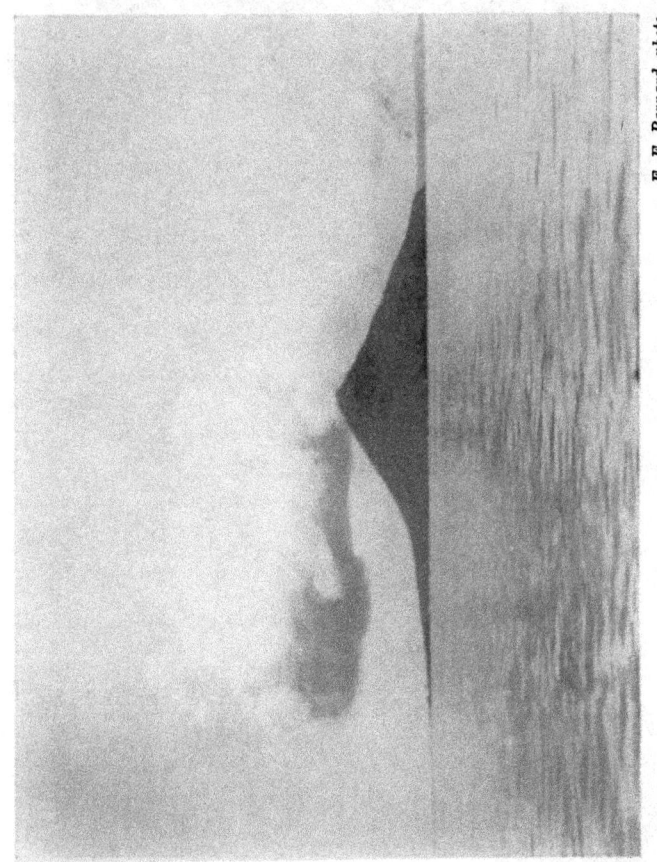

Fig. 45. hd. Cumulus, over Island. Krakatoa.

CLOUD FORMS

FIG. 46. Cumulus, Coast of Antarctica. British Antarctic Expedition, 1910-1913

Ponting, photo.

E. E. Barnard, photo.

FIG. 47. he. Cumulus, Towering. East End of Java

CLOUD FORMS 103

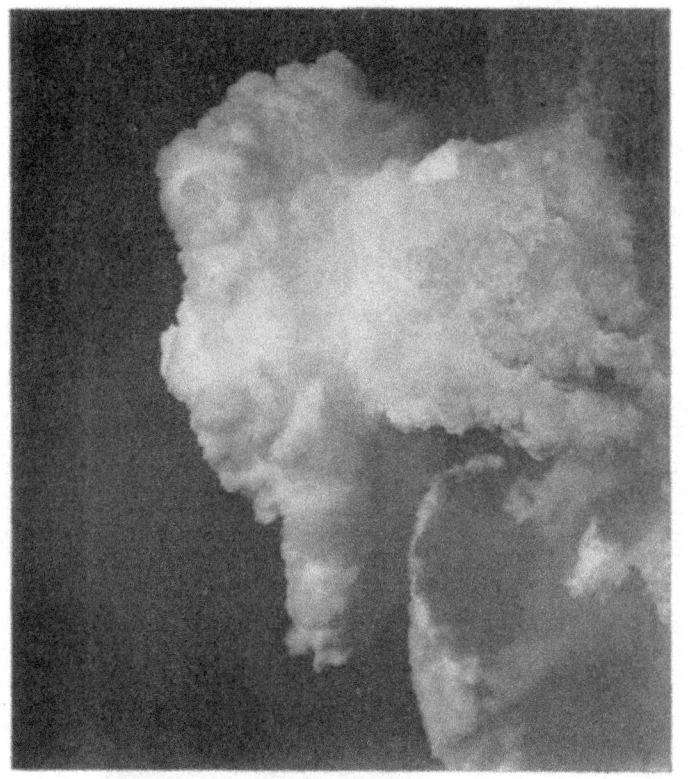

F. E. Barnard, photo.

FIG. 48. Cumulus, Mushrooming Head. Seen at Yerkes Observatory, Wisconsin

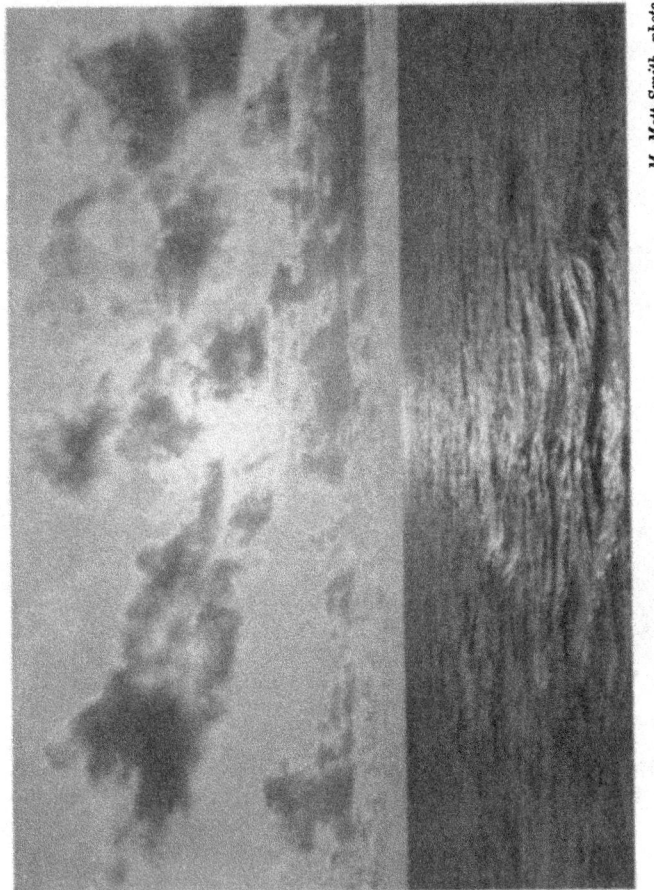

Fig. 49. ia. Fractocumulus

CLOUD FORMS 105

F. Ellerman, photo.

FIG. 50. ia. Fractocumulus; in denser Portions, Stratocumulus. Seen from Mount Wilson, Calif.

106 FOGS, CLOUDS AND AVIATION

W. J. Humphreys, photo.

FIG. 51. ia. Fractocumulus

F. Ellerman, photo.

FIG. 52. Cumulus Formed by Forest Fire. Seen from Mount Wilson, Calif.

O. H. Lawrence, photo.

Fig. 53. Cumulus Formed by Forest Fire on Sister Elsie Peak, Calif.

every 15 pounds of fuel burned, so that the fire cumulus is not entirely due to convection.

As just stated cumuli are formed only when the surface air is considerably warmer than that some distance above, this being essential to convection, but the absolute temperature need not be high. In fact cumuli occur even in polar regions. (Fig. 46.)

Since cumuli are caused by rising air currents induced by relatively high surface temperatures, they are very common in equatorial regions, and also through the middle latitudes during summer. Hence, too, they commonly occur over land most frequently during the afternoon and over water late at night. For the same reason they often follow a coast line, over the water at night and over the land through the day. Similarly they are common over islands (Fig. 45), whose presence frequently is shown in this way while they themselves are still below the horizon.

Scattering and comparatively small cumuli, especially those without well defined flat bases, are so common during fair weather that they often are called fair weather cumuli.

Cumuli, like other scattered clouds, are convenient

110 FOGS, CLOUDS AND AVIATION

hide-and-seek places for the aviator. The larger cumuli also show the places of ascending currents that sustain the glider.

9. *Cumulonimbus (Cunb.).*—*Heavy masses of cloud, with great vertical development, whosd cumuliform summits rise in the form of mountains or towers, the upper parts having a fibrous texture and often spreading out in the shape of an anvil.*

The base resembles nimbostratus, and one generally notices virga. This base has often a layer of very low ragged clouds below it.

"From the base local showers of rain or snow, occasionally of hail or soft hail [graupel], usually fall. Sometimes the upper margins have the compact shape of cumulus or form massive heaps, around which floats delicate false cirrus. At other times the margins themselves are fringed with filaments similar to cirrus clouds. This last form is particularly common with spring showers. The front of a thunderstorm of wide extent is frequently in the form of a large low arch above a region of uniformly lighter sky." (Figs. 54, 55, 56, 57, 58 and 59.)

This is the most turbulent and also the thickest of

CLOUD FORMS 111

FIG. 54. ja. Cumulonimbus. Seen from Mount Wilson, Calif.

F. Ellerman, photo.

112 FOGS, CLOUDS AND AVIATION

Fig. 55. ja. Cumulonimbus. Hailstorm over Pasadena, Calif.

F. Ellerman, photo.

CLOUD FORMS 113

FIG. 56. ja. Cumulonimbus. Seen from Mount Weather, Va.

A. J. Weed, photo.

114   FOGS, CLOUDS AND AVIATION

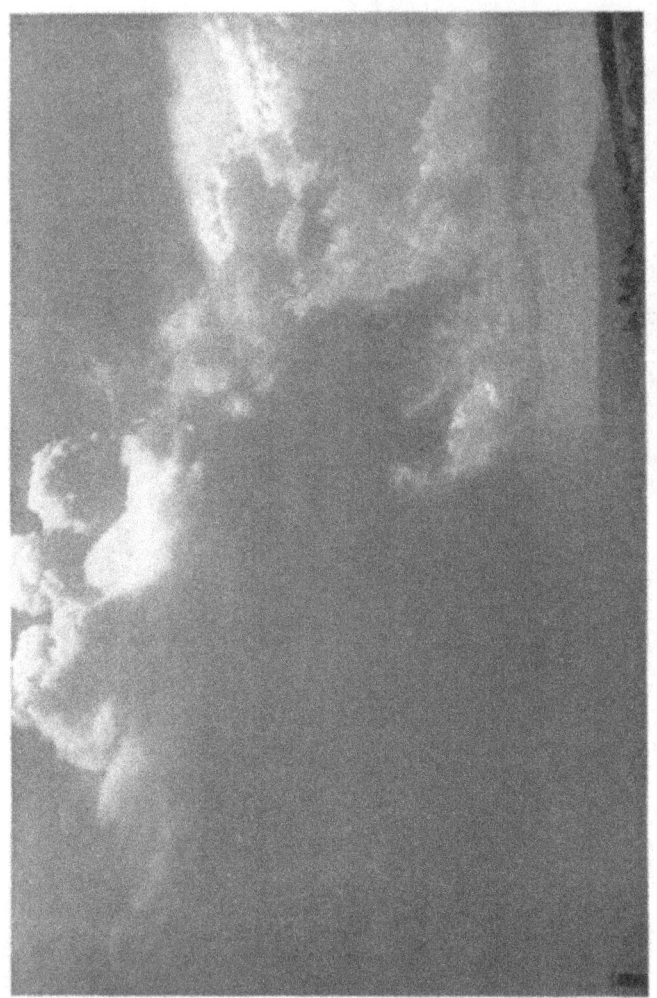

FIG. 57. ja. Cumulonimbus. Seen from Mount Weather, Va.

CLOUD FORMS 115

Fig. 58, ja. Cumulonimbus. Near Pensacola, Fla.

116   FOGS, CLOUDS AND AVIATION

Fig. 59. jb. Cumulonimbus, Showing the Storm Collar, Huntington, W. Va.

W. J. Humphreys, photo.

all clouds, ranging in depth commonly from 1 to 3 miles, and occasionally, in tropical regions, even to 8 or 9 miles. Its times, places, and modes of occurrence are all the same as those of the cumulus, given above.

10. Stratus (St.).—*A uniform layer of cloud, resembling fog, but not resting on the ground.*

"The cloud layer of stratus is always very low. If it is divided into ragged masses in a wind or by mountain tops it may be called *fractostratus*. The complete absence of detail of structure differentiates stratus from other aggregated forms of cloud." (Figs. 60 and 61.)

The stratus is the lowest of clouds, averaging around 2,000 feet above the surface. It frequently is formed by the lifting of relatively warm, humid air by underrunning cold winds; by the flow of a warm, humid wind over a surface stratum of cold air; and by the drifting of deep fog from the sea over relatively warm land, as in the case of the "velo" cloud of southern California, in which the lower portion of the fog is delightfully evaporated away, while the upper part is left as a gracious veil that shields one from the sun until nearly noon.

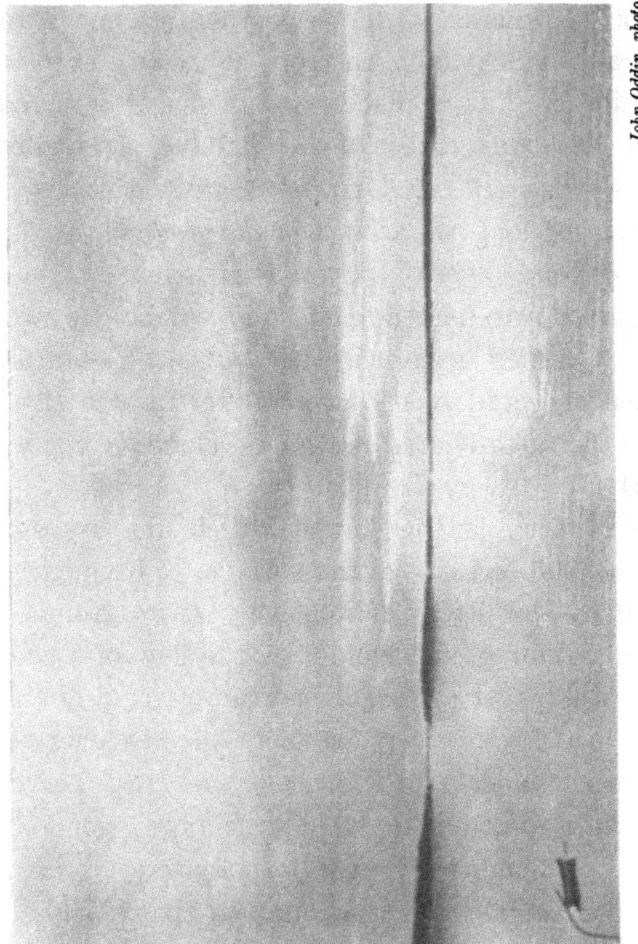

Fig. 60. ka. Stratus. Rockland, Me.

CLOUD FORMS 119

FIG. 61. kd. Stratus, above; Scud or Steam Cloud below. San Gabriel Range, Calif.

Notice should always be taken when the clouds seem motionless and also when they move with very great velocity.

SPECIAL CLOUD FORMS

It may seem, no doubt, that enough cloud forms have already been mentioned to include every type known to the heavens, and thus to satisfy the most ardent cloud observer, but, in addition to the gradual transformation of a cloud from one type to another, giving stages that puzzle the expert, there are several occasional forms sufficiently distinct, even though some of them belong to the general types already mentioned, to justify individual names and special descriptions.

Billow cloud.—Billow clouds (Fig. 62), also called windrow clouds and wave clouds, occur in nearly equally spaced parallel bands, generally with intervening strips of clear sky. The billow cloud most frequently, perhaps, is only a special form of the more general altocumulus. It also is a common form, rather as ripples, however, of the cirrocumulus (Fig. 27). On rare occasions it likewise occurs at low levels where it might be called a type of stratocumulus.

CLOUD FORMS 121

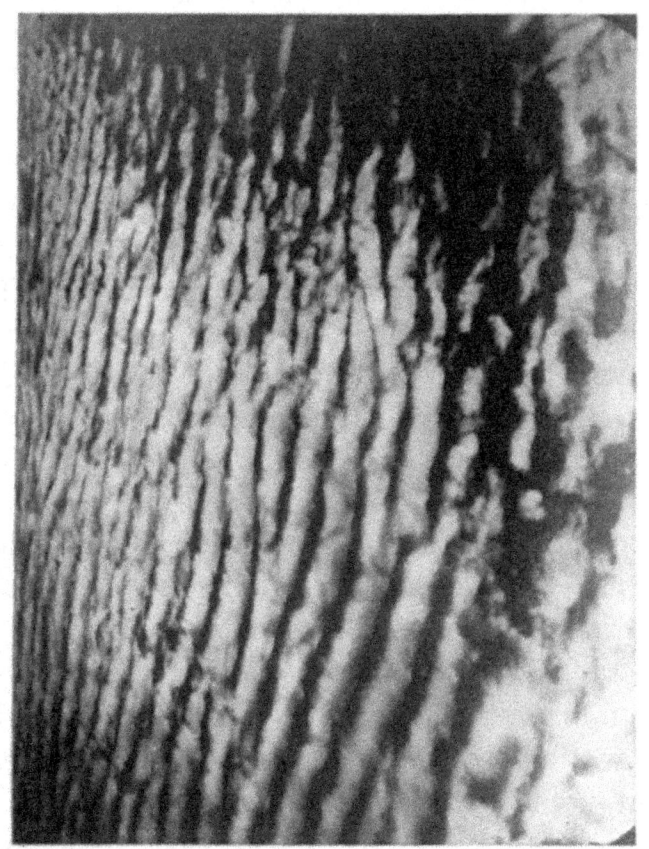

A. J. Henry, photo.

FIG. 62. da. Billow Cloud. A Form of Altocumulus

Billow clouds of the long wave-length type, those that are widely spaced, probably are formed by the flowing of one stratum or current of air over another of distinctly greater density, thereby creating air billows precisely as water billows are formed on the ocean. Now, the crests or tops of these waves are cooled by expansion, having risen above their previous level, and their troughs or bottoms warmed by compression. Hence, when the under layer is practically saturated, each crest, because of this cooling, is cloud-capped, and each trough clear, because relatively warm.

It is particularly interesting to note that although each billow cloud maintains its identity and position in the series of waves as long as it exists at all—for hours it may be—nevertheless the actual particles of which it consists at any instant have only the briefest duration, there being continuous condensation on the rising or windward side of the billow and equivalent evaporation in the descending or leeward portion.

Furthermore, while the billow cloud progresses steadily across the sky, its velocity is neither that of the upper stratum nor of the lower, any more than the velocity of a water wave is either that of the wind that is producing it or of the water in which it occurs. Wind velocity, therefore, can not be determined by measurements on clouds of this kind; nor, of course, by attempted measurements on any of the stationary types, such as those mentioned below.

Billow clouds of the short wave-length type, or those that are spaced close together, probably are formed by local convection through a shallow, unstable layer of saturated, or nearly saturated, air into a cross current above.

So far as practicable the aviator should keep either above or below a layer of billow clouds, since in their midst the air is likely to be quite bumpy.

Lenticular cloud.—The lenticular cloud (Figs. 63, 64, 65, 66, 67 and 68) often is only the cloud cap to a stationary or nearly stationary air billow produced as a rule by the flow of the wind over an uneven surface. It is especially common among high peaks and rugged mountains. Its material, like that of the crest cloud, is in rapid change—condensation on the windward side and evaporation to the leeward. Hence it is shaped like a double convex lens, the sug-

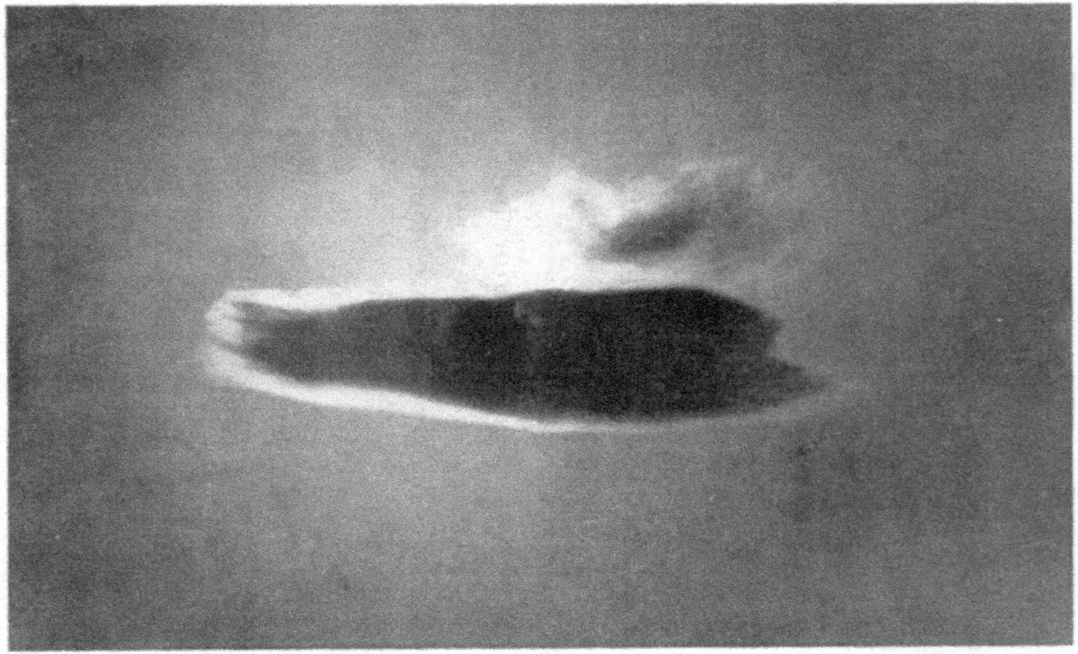

Fig. 63. 1a. Lenticular Cloud (Cumulus lenticularis)

C. F. Brooks, photo.

CLOUD FORMS 125

Fig. 64. 1b. Lenticular Cloud (Altocumulus lenticularis). 100 Miles North of Ottawa, Canada

Kindness New England Power Co.

Fig. 65. 1c. Lenticular Cloud. (Obstruction Cloud.) Over Mount Rainier, Washington

O. P. Anderson, photo.

CLOUD FORMS 127

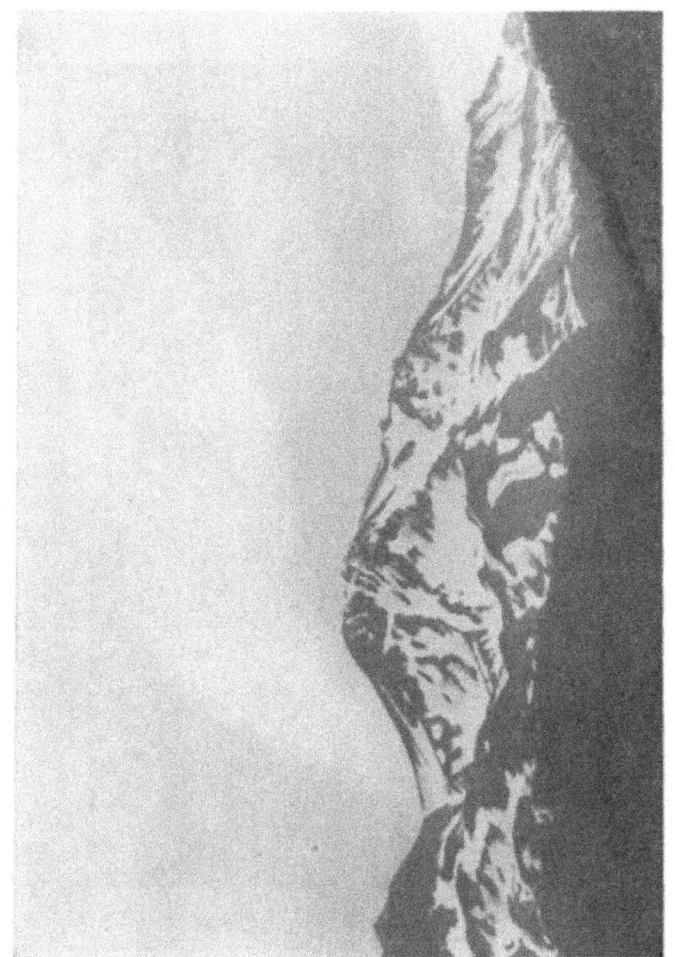

C. A. *Gilchrist, photo.*

FIG. 66. 1c. Lenticular Cloud (Obstruction Cloud). Over Mount Shasta, Calif.

Fig. 67. ld. Lenticular Cloud (Stratus lenticularis) below; Alto-stratus above. Seen from Mount Wilson, Calif.

F. Ellerman, photo.

CLOUD FORMS

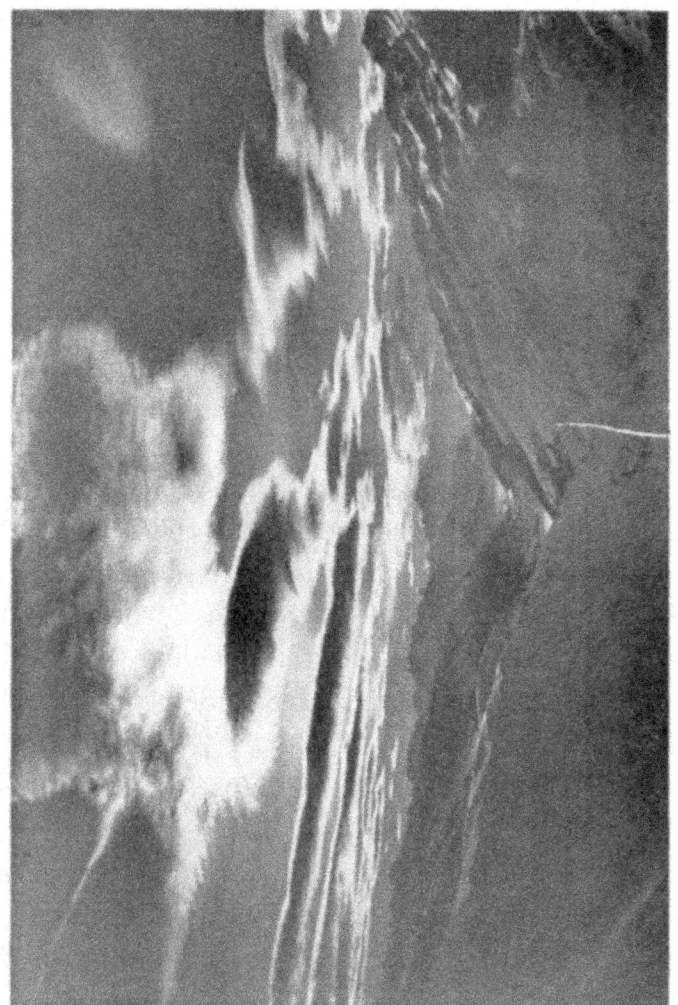

Jean Gaberell, photo.

FIG. 68. 1d. Lenticular Cloud (Stratus lenticularis) Among Swiss Alps

gestive origin of its name, thickest in the middle and thinning away to nothing on either side.

As implied above, frequently this is a stationary cloud, and hence one of the several that can not be used to measure wind velocities.

Crest cloud.—The crest cloud (Figs. 69, 70, 71 and 72) is caused by the upward deflection, and consequent cooling by expansion, of humid winds by a long mountain ridge, whose crest it commonly covers, whence its name, and whose sides it often gracefully drapes. Occasionally, however, it forms slightly above and a trifle to the leeward of the ridge along the topmost (hence coolest) portion of the deflected wind current. In either case the cloud is permanent in position only, being continuously created (condensed) on the windward or ascending and cooling side, and destroyed (evaporated) on the lee or descending and warming side.

The best known example, perhaps, of this interesting cloud is the celebrated "Table Cloth" (Fig. 72) of Cape Town pride, spread by the southeasterlies over the top and down the sides of Table Mountain.

When the obstruction is only a peak the crest cloud

CLOUD FORMS

Fig. 69. Crest Cloud. On Peters Mountain, W. Va.

W. J. Humphreys, photo.

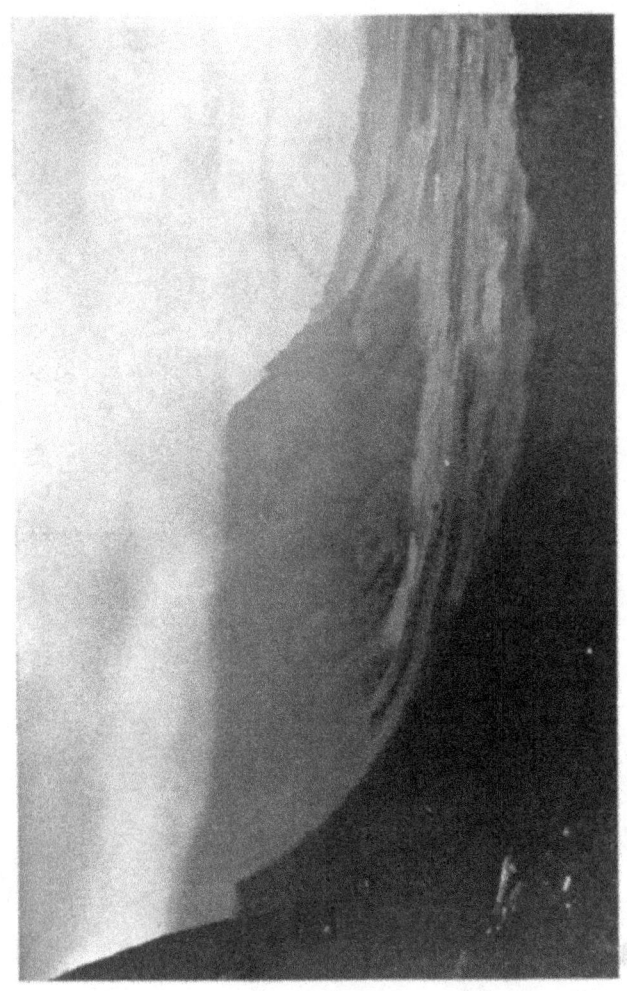

Fig. 70. Crest Cloud, Windward Side. Seen from the Pali, near Honolulu, H. I.

CLOUD FORMS 133

Fig. 71. Crest Cloud, Lee Side, Seen from Honolulu, H. I.

134   FOGS, CLOUDS AND AVIATION

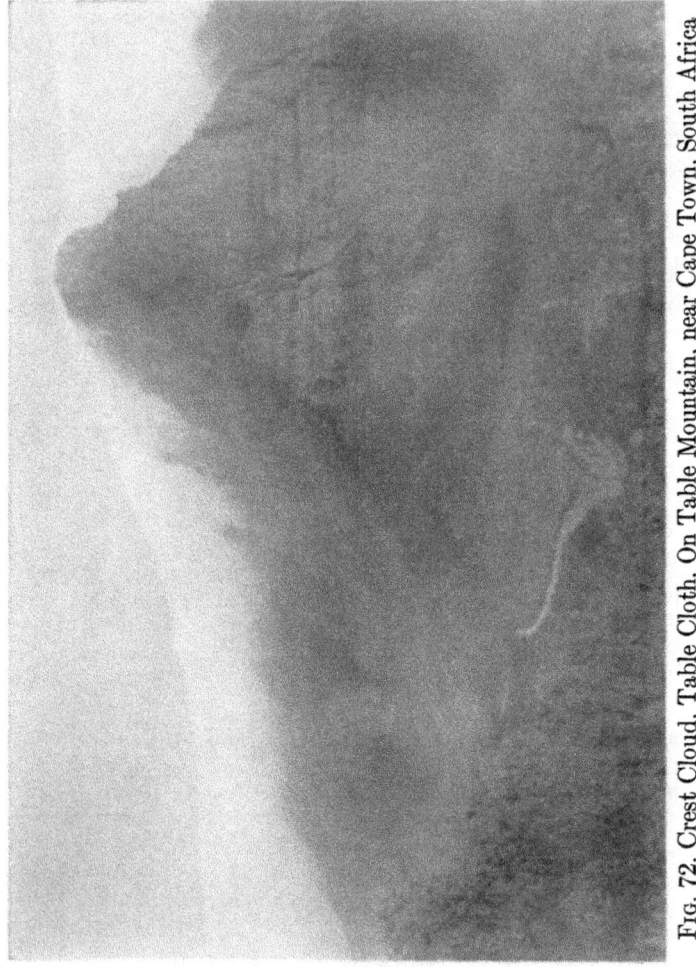

Fig. 72. Crest Cloud, Table Cloth. On Table Mountain, near Cape Town, South Africa

is apt to be called a cap, hat, cowl, hood, and the like, all of which are recognized signs of bad weather, as, for instance:

> When Falkland Hill puts on his cap,
> The Howe o'Fife will get a drap.
> When Traprain puts on his hat,
> The Lothian lads may look to that.
>
> When Rubenslaw puts on his cowl,
>   The Dunion on his hood,
> Then a'the wives of Teviotside
> Ken there will be a flood.

Riffle cloud.—Very often the crest cloud along a mountain ridge is paralleled by a similar but smaller cloud over the leeward valley, or plain in the case of the exceptional isolated mountain. The wind, deflected in a great wave over the mountain, rises in a series of decreasing billows beyond, like the waves or riffles in a river due to a ledge of rock, or other obstruction, on the bottom—hence the name "riffle cloud." A famous example of this cloud is the well known "helm bar" of northern England, so named because it was fancifully supposed to ward off (bar) the winds from the helmet cloud (crest cloud) of the Pennine mountains.

The process by which the crest cloud is formed along the ridge of the mountain and restricted thereto, that is, the cooling of the air by ascent on the windward side and its warming by descent on the lee side, occurs also in the rising and falling air on the windward and the lee sides respectively of the series of air waves, or giant riffles, induced by the mountain obstruction to the wind. Hence, when the crest cloud is at all heavy the top of the first and largest wave is apt to be clouded; even the second wave occasionally shows some cloud, but the third rarely if ever.

The crest cloud and the riffle cloud, since they show the presence of humid winds, are excellent signs of rain, or snow, in a few hours. The order of occurrence is: Formation of the crest cloud; thickening of the crest cloud and forming of the riffle cloud; growth and union of these two clouds and the complete covering of the sky; onset of rain or snow.

Banner cloud.—The banner cloud (Fig. 73) suggests a great white flag, whence its name, floating from a tall mountain peak. In strong winds the atmospheric pressure to the immediate leeward of such a peak is more or less reduced. If the humidity

CLOUD FORMS 137

C. D. Walcott, photo.

FIG. 73. Banner Cloud. On Mount Assiniboine, Canada

is right this causes a cloud through the resulting cooling, aided, no doubt, in many cases, by the cold walls of the peak itself. In many cases it may consist largely, or even wholly, of drifting snow. Here too, as in the preceding cases, the cloud is stationary, but its substance in rapid flux through condensation on one side and evaporation on the other.

Cumulus boa, boa cumulus, or *boa.*—Many a high mountain peak, when the air grows damp, wraps about itself a "boa" of delicate texture, exquisite design, and appropriately gigantic size. (Figs. 74 and 75.) Such is the *serpe* (serpent) of the Italians, seen for ages on the sides of Mount Etna and properly regarded as a harbinger of rain. It is a stream of low cumulus that flows from the fountain of cloud produced by the upward deflection of humid air on the windward slopes—air that, like water, and for much the same reason, flows not over an obstacle, but around it, if there be a way, carrying along in this case its flood-drift of cloud.

The name, or, at least, characterizing term "boa," an international word, is given to this cloud because of its striking resemblance to the well known boa of comfort and adornment.

CLOUD FORMS 139

FIG. 74. Cumulus boa (Boa cloud). Along Mount Pilatus, Switzerland

140 FOGS, CLOUDS AND AVIATION

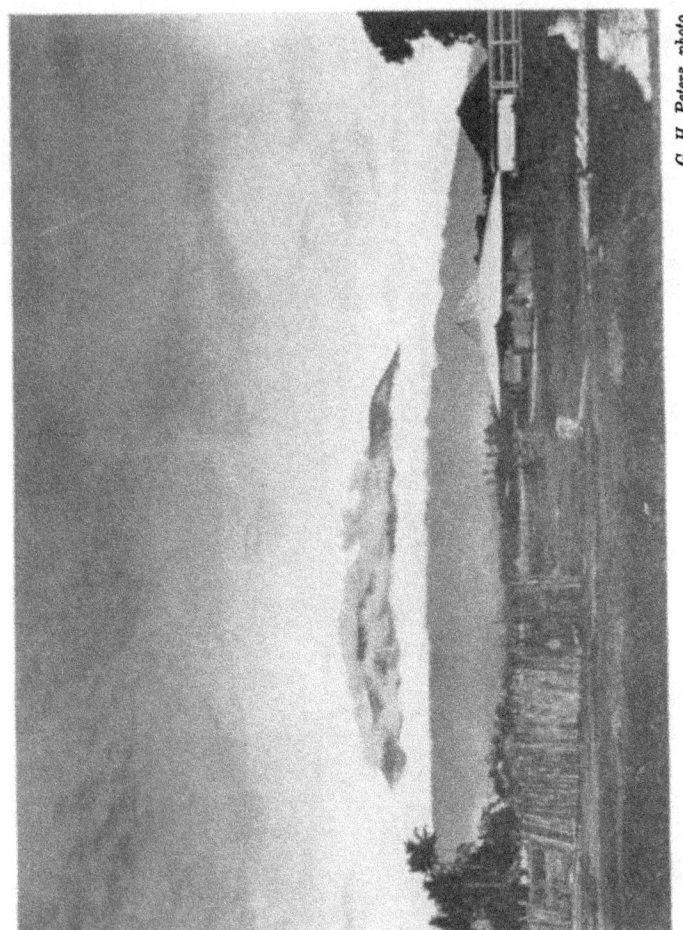

Fig. 75. Cumulus boa. Mount Merapi, Sumatra

G. H. Peters, photo.

Scarf cloud.—It occasionally happens that as a cumulus rises rapidly to a great height a thin cirrus-like cloud arch, convex upward, forms above, and detached from, the topmost cumulus head (Fig. 76), so suggestive of a halo as to arouse poetic if not even pious fancies. As the cumulus continues to rise this flossy cloud grows and rests like a veil over the thunderhead. A little later, a few minutes at most, it mantles the cumulus shoulder (Fig. 77), the head or heads being free, and may even drape the sides. In all cases it has the sheen and apparent texture of a great silken scarf—hence the name. It has often been called false cirrus, but that term is now commonly restricted to an entirely different cloud. It frequently is also called a cap cloud, but this name, apart from being loosely applied to any sort of cloud on a mountain peak, is applicable, by analogy, only during the early stages of the development of the scarf cloud and hence neither distinctive nor properly descriptive.

It is caused by the rising and consequent expansion and cooling of the air directly above the cumulus heads. Ordinarily this movement and cooling of the

FIG. 76. Scarf Cloud (over Cumulus). Above Mount Shasta, Calif.

CLOUD FORMS

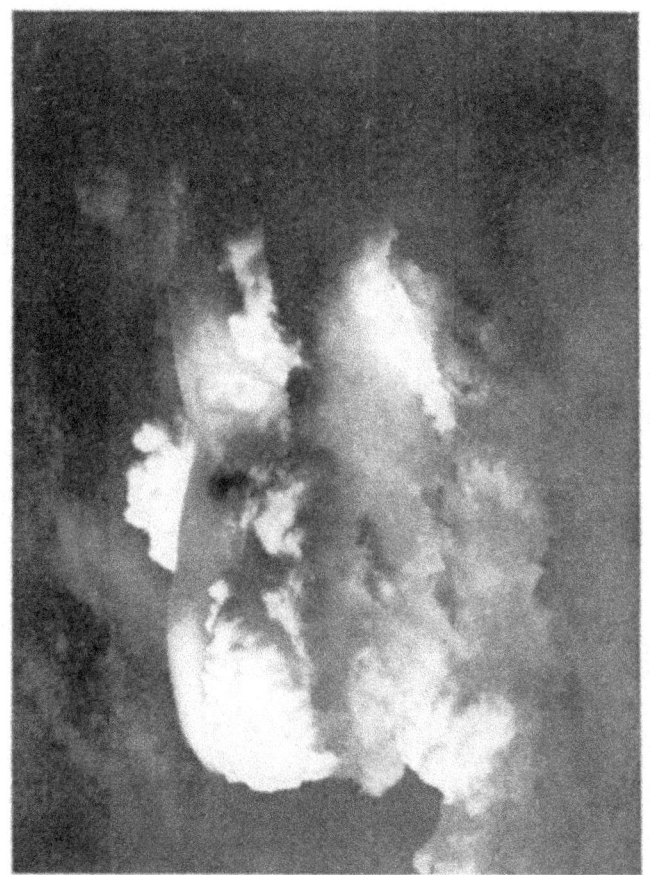

W. A. Bentley, photo.

FIG. 77. Scarf Cloud (Resting on Cumulus)

air over the cumulus produces no visible effect, but occasionally, there happens to be a stratum of air at a considerable height (3 or 4 miles) that is practically saturated, and when such a layer is lifted locally, as just explained, a thin cloud, the first stage of the scarf cloud, is formed at the place of disturbance. When this layer is thin, as it commonly is, the thunderheads generally pass quite through it into drier air above, leaving the scarf cloud mantling the shoulders of the cumulus, or draping its sides at about the original level of the humid stratum.

Although this is not a rare cloud, and a fair indicator of local thunder showers, few, apparently, are familiar with it, owing to its ephemeral nature and occurrence with other clouds. It has, of course, but little of the grandeur of a towering cumulus or intricacy of a far-flung cirrus, nevertheless, its coming into existence at an unexpected place, its silken texture, and its changes in form and position all merit its being carefully looked for and closely followed when found.

Tonitro-cirrus.—The name "tonitro-cirrus," thunder cirrus, is applied to those gray locks, to speak figuratively, combed out from old thunderheads by the upper winds, and also the thinner edges of the *anvil cloud*, or spreading top of a cumulonimbus. (Figs. 78 and 79.)

Even though the winds of the lower atmosphere are always light when great towering cumuli are formed, the upper winds may still be strong. Clearly, then, the top of a cumulus that extends into a stratum of swift winds is certain to be drawn out into a more or less extensive, fibrous sheet of snow crystals that differs but little, if any, from the ordinary cirrus except in its mode of origin. A more common name for this cloud is "false cirrus," but this term is objectionable since the cloud in question is indeed a cirrus, differing from other cirri, as stated, only in origin.

Mammato-cumulus.—The mammatocumulus, called also pocky-cloud, festoon-cloud, sack-cloud, "rain balls," and several other local names, is a sort of miniature up-side-down cumulus. (Figs. 80 and 81.) It occurs most frequently in connection with severe thunderstorms, and appears to be due to irregular descents here and there of cold air onto an existing stratus cloud, each place of fall being marked by a downward bulge in the cloud base.

Tornado or funnel cloud.—The tornado or funnel

FIG. 78. Tonitro-cirrus (False Cirrus). Drawn out from Anvil Cloud, over Valley of Virginia

A. J. Weed, photo.

CLOUD FORMS

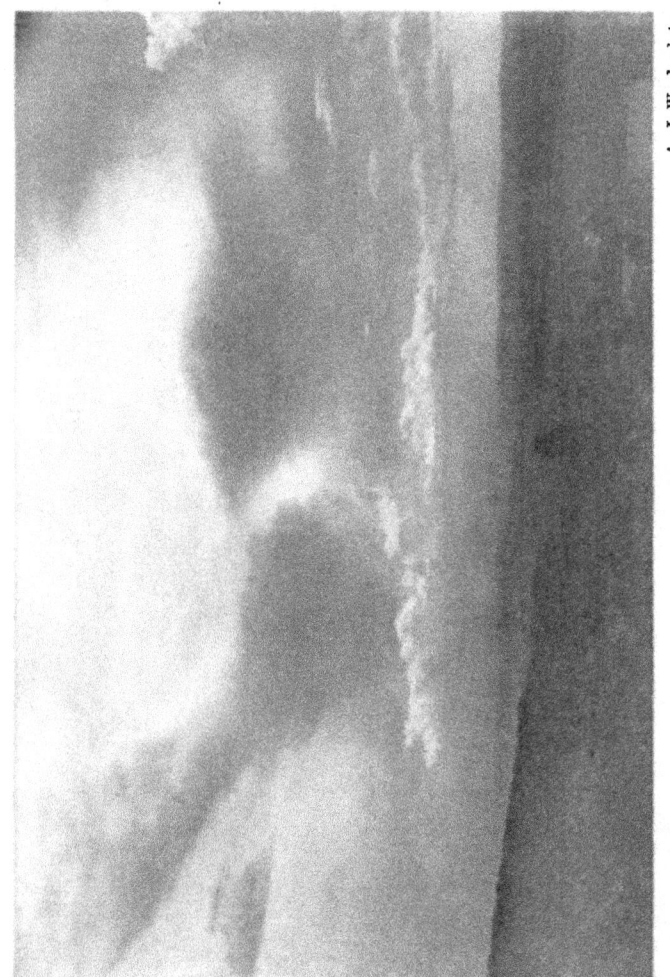

A. J. Weed, photo.

Fig. 79. Tonitro-Cirrus (False Cirrus) above; Cumulonimbus below. Over Valley of Virginia

148   FOGS, CLOUDS AND AVIATION

Fig. 80. Mammatocumulus. Ashland, Ky. Taken Just Before Fig. 81, and Showing Much of Same Cloud

W. J. Humphreys, photo.

Fig. 81. Mammatocumulus. Ashland, Ky. Taken Just After Fig. 80, and Showing Much of Same Cloud

W. J. Humphreys, photo.

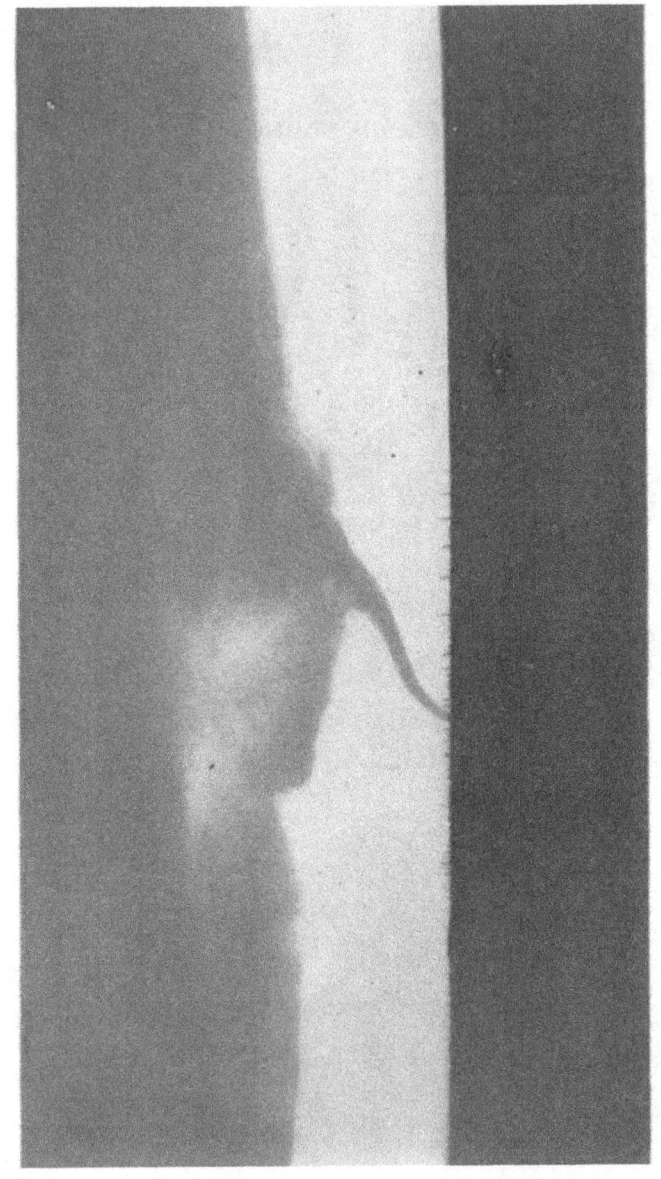

Fig. 82. Funnel Cloud (Tornado Cloud). Near Elmwood, Neb., April 6, 1919

W. A. Wood, photo.

G. B. *Pickwell, photo*

FIG. 83. Funnel Cloud (Tornado Cloud). From two Exposures Taken close Together, Upper one First. Seen near Elmwood, Neb., April 6, 1919

Fig. 84. Funnel Cloud (Tornado Cloud), Solomon, Kans.

cloud (Figs. 82, 83 and 84) is only a long funnel-shaped cloud about the axis of rotation of a tornado. It hangs down, either straight or curved, from the base of a rain cloud—commonly, if not always, a cumulonimbus—and varies in extent all the way from a mere protuberance on the parent cloud, to a crooked trunk reaching all the way to the earth. It is caused by the cooling, due to expansion, of the rotating air, to a temperature below the dew-point. In short, it is just cloud, induced, like other clouds, by cooling, though often mixed with dust in its lower portion.

Waterspout.—The well-known waterspout, in the sense of the visible part of the vortical storm, is only a funnel cloud over water, generally smaller than that over land but otherwise quite the same, except that its base is filled with spray instead of dust and debris.

Chapter IV
CLOUD MISCELLANY

As the devil said to Noah, "It's bound to clear up."

CLOUD MATERIAL

Clouds consist either of water droplets, always when the temperature is above freezing, or ice crystals, normally when the temperature is below freezing, but not invariably, because occasionally the droplets cool without solidifying to, or, perhaps, form at, temperatures far below the "freezing point."

The droplets that together constitute a cloud out of which no rain is falling vary in size from the vanishingly small, especially at the surface and edges where they are likely to be disappearing by evaporation, or coming into existence through condensation, up to several fold that of the average particle. Most of them, however, appear to be about one one-thousandth of an inch in diameter, roughly the size of the familiar lycopodium spore. In rain clouds, on the other hand, such as the cumulonimbus, this range is much greater—from the invisibly minute, as before, up to the fully developed drop of one-tenth, say, to one-fifth (the maximum possible) of an inch across.

The ice crystals, the material of cold clouds, also vary widely in size, and include every gradation from the minute, almost microscopic, needles of the cirrus to the well-known snow flakes of the winter storm. Their chief claim, however, on our attention is not because of this interesting dimensional range, but owing to their exquisite beauty. The fundamental pattern, however simple or complex the crystal, is always the same, the hexagon, or six-sided column, but the variety is endless: Needles with pyramidal ends; columns, (Fig. 85), with flat ends; mere hexagonal flakes, hexagons with a simple extension at each angle, and hexagons with complex extensions in myriad varieties—and all are beautiful. Naturally then, hundreds of these numberless forms, as admirably photographed by that enthusiast, the late Mr. W. A. Bentley, of Jericho, Vt., have been used as models in design and art. Nor has there been a keener zest than Mr. Bentley's as year after year he added pattern upon pattern to his long since marvelous collection of photomicrographs of the snow crystal.

W. A. Bentley, photo.

Fig. 85. Snow Crystals

WHY THE ATMOSPHERE AS A WHOLE NEVER IS SATURATED

Since evaporation is continuous from much the greater portion of the surface of the earth, it would seem that the atmosphere would soon become saturated throughout, and perhaps even filled everywhere with fog and cloud. But before the surface air has become approximately saturated to any considerable depth it commonly is carried to higher levels by some type of convection, and this causes it to cool, as already explained, and eventually to give up much of its moisture, generally in the condition of rain or snow. Sooner or later, however, the air out of which the precipitation falls returns to lower levels where clearly it is less humid, on the average, than when it began to ascend, by the amount of water abandoned during its upward course. In short, vertical convection induces precipitation through cooling, and precipitation in turn so dries the air as to prevent it from becoming and remaining everywhere intolerably humid, as it otherwise would be.

WHY CLOUDS FLOAT

Since water is about 800 times heavier than air, one might well wonder how it is possible for a cloud, consisting of myriads of droplets, to float in a medium so light and of such slight resistance to penetration as the atmosphere. But, however imperceptible and entirely negligible the resistance of still air may be to our own movements, it is not strictly zero. In vacuo, for instance, as we know from one of the most familiar of experiments, "the farthing and the feather fall together," but more and more apart in air of increasing density. Now the total pull of a raindrop, say, causing it to fall, remains the same no matter how finely it is divided, while the amount of air disturbed, and hence the resistance and time of fall, increase with every subdivision; and since a single raindrop, one-sixth of an inch in diameter, is divisible into, or is the equivalent of, 8,000,000 average cloud droplets, it is clear that, while the rain may descend, the cloud must settle, if it comes down at all, much more slowly.

Cloud droplets of the size just implied—that is, such that 1,200 of them side by side make a row 1 inch long—do, as a matter of fact, fall through still air about 8 feet per minute. Hence, where there are no rising currents, a cloud must, and does, gradually sink into the lower unsaturated air and evaporate.

Clouds, however, as explained above, commonly are formed in ascending currents, and this ascent generally is distinctly greater than 8 feet per minute, the rate just given of cloudfall in still air. Hence cloud is continuously formed at that level at which the rising air is cooled by its expansion to the dew point. The droplets here formed are carried to higher levels, there evaporated or merged into raindrops, or carried away, or spread out at the convectional limit, or "ceiling," as it is called, as circumstances determine, but new droplets replacing these are as continuously being formed as fresh humid air rises to the cloud level.

Clouds, therefore, do not even eventually fall to the earth because either they are continuously formed at the condensation level by rising currents or, on slowly sinking (8 feet per minute) to lower levels in still air, or being dragged down by descending air, are soon evaporated. In any case the cloud floats at a greater or less height and never falls precipitately to the earth as does rain.

HOW RAIN IS PRODUCED

Few people ever ask how rain is produced. Perhaps this is because the phenomenon is too familiar to arouse one's curiosity or make him in the least inquisitive. Nevertheless, and however childish it may seem, it is both a rational question and a difficult one to answer.

The familiar, pretended answer, is, in effect, that somehow the air is cooled until condensation occurs on the various nuclei present, and that the larger of the droplets thus produced that happen to be well up in the cloud fall to lower levels, thereby encountering many other particles and through coalescence with them growing into full-sized drops. But, as implied, this explanation explains nothing. In the first place there are so many nuclei present in the atmosphere— hundreds at least, and usually thousands, to every cubic inch—that division of the condensed vapor between them leaves every one quite too minute to fall with any considerable velocity. Then, too, calculation shows that if a particle should fall, in the manner supposed, through a cloud even a mile thick and pick up everything in its path it still would be a small drop. That is, rain is not formed in this simple manner, as is also obvious from the fact that a cloud may last for many hours without giving any rain whatever.

The actual processes in the formation of rain seem to be:

1. For some reason, such as surface heating, a mountain in the wind's path, or convergence of different currents, the surface air is forced up to considerable heights; during which rise it does work—gives up energy—by expansion against the surrounding pressure and thereby cools.

2. As soon as the dew point is passed condensation begins on the innumerable nuclei present and a cloud is formed, the particles of which, being heavier than equal volumes of air, slowly fall with reference to the atmosphere itself. That is, the rising current passes by the cloud particles to a greater or less extent however high they may be carried.

3. The lower cloud particles filter the air rising through them and thereby more or less clean it of dust motes and other nuclei. Hence the droplets formed in the rising air after this filtration grow much faster, being relatively few, than they otherwise would.

4. Presently many of the larger droplets coalesce and thus become heavy enough to fall against the

rising current. Nor, indeed, can they fall (reach lower levels) until by condensation, or coalescence, or both, they have attained a certain minimum size determined by the vertical velocity of the air in which they happen to be.

In short, a rising current, essential to any considerable condensation, that sustains, or even carries higher, cloud droplets until they have grown to falling size, and the automatic filtering of the ascending air by the cloud formed in it (which filtering restricts further condensation to comparatively few particles and thus insures their rapid growth), appear to be necessary and sufficient to account for the formation of rain.

5. Most of the drops, as they emerge from a cloud, are likely to have substantially the same size, namely, that which is just sufficient to overcome the upward movement of the air in which they were formed. Now, drops of the same size fall with the same speed, hence any two that happen to be close together are likely to remain so much longer than drops of unequal size and thereby have more chances of union through fortuitous disturbances. Furthermore, when falling

drops are side by side the air tends to push them together just as passing boats are forced toward each other. Clearly, though, this pressure has time to bring closely neighboring drops into actual contact only when they fall with the same or very nearly the same speed. From these considerations it seems that the smallest drops, size 1, say, should unite to form size 2, and size 2 unite with each other to form size 4, rather than with size 1 to form size 3, and so on, doubling at each union. Hence we should expect more drops having the weights 1, 2, 4, 8, . . .than any intermediate values, and this expectation has been fully verified by observations on all sorts of rains.

MEASURING CLOUD HEIGHTS

It is always interesting and sometimes very useful to know the heights of the clouds, or, to be more exact, the heights of their bases—useful, frequently, to the aviator to whom very low clouds may be a danger and certainly a nuisance, and useful as an aid in forecasting the local weather for the next few hours.

There are several methods of determining the heights of clouds as accurately as ever is necessary.

Indeed, under favorable circumstances, the error may not be more than a few feet.

1. The aviator, for instance, can take the reading, corrected if necessary, of his altimeter the instant he climbs into the base of a cloud.

2. A pilot balloon (small free balloon without instruments) may be observed from two stations a mile, say, apart, and its exact direction from each station, both horizontal and vertical, noted as it disappears into a cloud base. From these directions, which can be determined very accurately with suitable theodolites, and from the known distance between the two observing stations and the height of either above the other, the cloud height is readily obtained by a simple trigonometrical calculation.

3. Any definite spot on the base of a cloud may be simultaneously observed (triangulated, to be exact) from two stations and its height calculated from the data thus obtained, precisely as in the case of the pilot balloon. The observations, of course, may be either visual or photographic; the latter, if well done, generally being the better since it affords opportunity for detailed study and independent measurements on many different points.

CLOUD MISCELLANY 165

4. The angular altitude of a kite and the length of wire out, at the time it enters a cloud base, also furnish a fair means of computing the desired height.

5. The exact time of disappearance of a kite up into a cloud may be noted, and the height of the kite at that instant, and hence also of the cloud, determined by subsequent examination of the temperature and pressure records on the kite instruments.

6. The level of storm clouds, or low clouds at the time of strong winds, and of ordinary cumuli, can be tolerably closely computed from the current values of the surface temperature and humidity.

The above are by no means all the possible ways of measuring the heights of clouds, but they are the more accurate and the ones most commonly practiced.

WHY THE BASE OF A GIVEN CLOUD, OR CLOUD SYSTEM, HAS EVERYWHERE NEARLY THE SAME HEIGHT

One of the most interesting and significant things learned from cloud measurements is the fact that the base of any cloud sheet—that is, a particular sheet at a particular time, whether continuous or broken and scattered—is everywhere at about the same level. The reasons for this are very simple: (*a*) Since the temperature and humidity of the air at any given time are nearly the same at neighboring places over a considerable area, the height throughout such region is approximately constant at which rising air will have cooled to the dew point and cloud begun to form. Hence the base levels of a series of detached cumulus clouds are about the same. (b) Since rising air ascends until by expansion it has cooled to the temperature of the then surrounding air, at which level it spreads out and drifts away with the general circulation, and as convection, whatever its cause, applies to air of all degrees of humidity, and occurs at different times and all manner of places, it follows that the atmosphere is always more or less stratified in respect to its water vapor. In general, therefore, clouds must also form in these layers. There may be, and often are, two or more cloud layers at the same time at different levels, but a cloud filling the whole depth of the atmosphere, or even a layer 5 or 6 miles thick, is not to be expected, nor is any such layer of considerable extent often formed.

LEVELS OF MAXIMUM CLOUDINESS

Since several types of clouds occur at various elevations, and since no level, from the surface of the earth up to the highest cirrus, is free from condensation, it might seem that clouds are as likely to have one height as another throughout their possible range. However, it is certain that there are levels of maximum and minimum cloud frequency, even though it may not be easy to prove some of them by direct observation owing to the prevalence of lower clouds. The more important levels of maximum cloudiness are:

Fog level.—As every one knows, a fog, whatever its depth, from a mere gauzy veil to the deepest and densest layer, is a cloud on the earth. Obviously, therefore, the surface of the earth itself is a level of maximum cloudiness.

Cumulus level.—Since evaporation tends all the time to saturate the atmosphere, and since humidity is held down by convectional condensation, and, further, since over extensive areas, convection is roughly the same most of the time through an entire season, it follows that the ordinary rain cloud, and the common cumulus cloud, must have a roughly standard base level at a moderate elevation. This level, therefore, say, 4,000 feet above the surface, is also a level of maximum cloudiness.

Altocumulus level.—The strong convection common to dry summer weather often produces small cumulus clouds at a considerable heights—frequently 2 to $2\frac{1}{2}$ miles above the surface. Furthermore, during the average thunderstorm a great deal of humidity is urged up to roughly this same level, and there spread out into a wide layer by the swifter winds of that height. Subsequent convections in this layer often induce many small cumuli. For both reasons, therefore, this level, known as the altocumulus level, is likewise one of maximum frequency of cloud.

Cirrostratus level.—The topmost portions of the clouds in a cyclonic, or general, rain are carried forward over very extensive areas by probably the swiftest winds of the entire atmosphere. Hence this level, roughly 5 miles above the surface, is also one of maximum cloud frequency, or at least of cloud observation.

Cirrus level.—Rising masses of air can not ascend beyond the level of the highest cirrus clouds: that is, in middle latitudes, above an elevation of about 6 or 7 miles. The reason for this is given below, under the caption: "Why there are no clouds above the high cirrus." Any air that reaches this level necessarily spreads out in an extensive sheet or layer in which, under favorable conditions, condensation occurs in the form of fine snow crystals. Hence this ultimate level of the ascending air, at which its horizontal spread is great, is also one of maximum cloud extent.

LEVELS OF MINIMUM CLOUDINESS

If there are different levels of maximum cloudiness, it follows that between each two such adjacent levels there must be a level of minimum cloudiness. However, there is nothing of particular interest about any of these intermediate levels.

WHY THERE ARE NO CLOUDS ABOVE THE HIGH CIRRUS

The region above the high cirrus also is one of minimum cloudiness. In fact clouds do not occur in that region at all, and the reason is as follows:

There clearly is some temperature (actually about 60°F. below zero) at which each portion of the high atmosphere must lose as much heat by radiation as it gains, and this the lowest temperature to which the free air can cool. This temperature is reached, in middle latitudes, at about 6 to 7 miles above sea level. Hence this is the limit of vertical convection—for higher convection would mean lower temperatures—and the maximum height, therefore, to which water vapor is carried. Of course some water vapor reaches greater heights by the slow process of diffusion, but all of this region is subject to frequent temperature changes—changes only a few days apart—just as is the lower atmosphere, hence as soon as any appreciable amount of vapor diffuses to a higher level than that of the average cirrus it is largely removed by the next cool wave in invisibly small amounts and the whole of the upper air thereby kept too dry for the formation of even the thinnest clouds.

RELATION OF CLOUD HEIGHTS TO SEASON

Clouds generally are lower during winter than during summer. This is because the relative humidity is higher, or the atmosphere more nearly saturated, during the colder season than during the warmer. And this condition, in turn, is owing largely to the fact that vertical convection, which is the chief cause of rain and hence the chief drying agency of the air, is most active during summer, when the surface of the earth is strongly heated.

RELATION OF CLOUD HEIGHTS TO LATITUDE

Just as clouds generally are higher in summer and lower in winter, so, too, and for the same reason, clouds commonly are highest in equatorial regions and gradually descend with increase of latitude to their lowest level in polar regions.

RELATION OF TYPE OF CLOUD TO THE SEASON

As just explained, vertical convection, which is owing largely to surface heating, is much stronger during summer than during winter. Hence the cumulus or woolpack cloud, a product of local convection, is characteristic of warm summer days, while the low stratus or layer cloud is equally characteristic of the winter season.

RELATION OF TYPE OF CLOUD TO LATITUDE

For the same reason that the prevailing type of cloud varies with the season, it also varies with latitude. That is, in tropical regions, where vertical convection is strong, the cumulus cloud is very common, whereas, in the high latitude regions, where convection is feeble, it is unusual. Here the prevailing cloud is of the stratus or layer type.

CLOUD THICKNESS

The thickness of clouds varies from all but zero in the case of faint cirrus, and vanishing wisps and flecks of any other type, up to the 10 miles or more from bottom to top of the towering tropical cumulo-nimbus. (Fig. 47.) Habitually, however, the high cirrus, only a few hundred feet thick, is the thinnest of clouds; and the cumulonimbus, especially when the seat of a hail storm, the thickest—often several miles deep. The common stratonimbus cloud, from which rain often falls all day, varies in thickness from, say, 500 feet, up to 4 or 5 miles. Its average thickness, however, appears to be, roughly, half a mile. All other types of clouds generally are intermediate in thickness between the cirrus and the nimbus, averaging, perhaps, 500 to 1,500 feet.

CLOUD VELOCITY

The direction and speed of travel of clouds can be determined in several ways, most of which involve triangulation of the kind used by surveyors and geologists. In the great majority of cases the velocity of a cloud is that of the air in which it happens to be. In a few cases, however, the movement of the cloud is not that of its enveloping atmosphere. Thus the cloud that forms along the crest of a mountain is as stationary as a waterfall, and, like the waterfall, is continually renewed by fresh material. No matter how swift the current, the fall remains fixed, and however strong the wind over the mountain, cloud is formed in it as soon as it reaches a particular altitude, determined by the humidity and temperature, and evaporated as it is drifted beyond and to lower levels. The crest cloud, therefore, being always stationary, can not be used in measuring wind velocity. Neither can the riffle cloud, the lenticular cloud, nor the banner cloud, and for the same reason—all except certain kinds of the lenticular, are stationary whatever the wind velocity.

Neither can the velocity of the wind be determined by the movement of the parallel rolls of the windrow or billow cloud. These clouds rest on the crests of air waves which are caused by the flow of one wind sheet over another. The velocity of these waves, and, hence, of the clouds that crest them, is intermediate between that of the two sheets and therefore does not measure the actual velocity of either.

In the great majority of cases, though—that is,

with the above exceptions—clouds do move strictly with the enveloping air. Hence, though everywhere blowing, in the course of time, from all directions—"boxing the compass," as the mariner says—in the Tropics they are nearly always from easterly points, northeast to southeast, and in middle latitudes prevailingly from westerly regions.

Their average velocity *when moving in their prevailing direction* increases with height at approximately the same proportion that the density of the atmosphere decreases—that is, at such a rate that the velocity of cloud or wind multiplied by the density of the air gives the same product for all heights, or, in short is a constant.

VARIATION OF CLOUDINESS WITH LATITUDE

As is well known, the amount of cloudiness varies greatly in different parts of the world. In some places it would be perfectly safe, following the example of the Yuma Hotel, to advertise free meals for every day the sun does not shine, and equally safe in others to make a similar offer for every whole day that it does. Apart from such obvious causes of cloud variation as direction of the wind, particularly onshore and offshore, elevation, temperature, etc., there is also a well-marked latitude effect. Thus, in the equatorial regions, where convection is most active, nearly 60 per cent, on the average, of the sky is clouded; around latitude 30°, both north and south, or along the great belts of high pressure and over the principal arid regions, the average cloudiness falls to the minimum value of 40 to 45 per cent, while in the neighborhood of the polar regions it becomes 60 to 75 per cent. All these are only average values for the respective latitudes. The cloudiness of individual places covers a much wider variation.

CLOUDS AS WEATHER SIGNS

Since the height, extent, and shape of clouds depend upon the humidity, temperature, and motion of the atmosphere, it is obvious that they often may furnish helpful hints of the coming weather. Thus, thin cirrus clouds, when not increasing in extent nor growing denser, indicate fair weather for at least 24 hours; and the same is true of the altocumuli. In general

"The higher the clouds, the finer the weather."

On the other hand, when the cirrus grows denser, and when the sky is covered with cirrocumuli, rain within 24 hours is likely.

> Mackerel scales and mares' tails
> Make lofty ships carry low sails.

Also, when large cumuli develop in the forenoon, there probably will be local thunder-showers in the afternoon.

> In the morning mountains,
> In the evening fountains.

Again, when two or more layers of cloud are moving in different directions, foul weather is almost certain to occur very soon. In short,

> Whene'er the clouds do weave
> 'Twill storm before they leave.

Clouds of the lower and intermediate levels from north to west usually imply fair weather for a day or two; clouds from east to south generally mean rain within 24 hours. (This is for most of the temperate regions of the Northern Hemisphere; for the Southern Hemisphere, write north for south and south for north.)

> When the carry [current of clouds] goes west,
> Gude weather is past;
> When the carry goes east
> Gude weather comes nest.

Fog clearing up early means a fair day; fog persisting implies that there probably will be rain later in the day, or during the coming night. As the proverb puts it:

> Mists dispersing on the plain
> Scatter away the clouds and rain;
> But when they hang on the mountain tops
> They'll soon descend in copious drops.

Chapter V

CLOUD SPLENDORS

I bind the sun's throne with a burning zone,
And the moon's with a girdle of Pearl.
—Shelley, *The Cloud*.

CREPUSCULAR RAYS

Everyone is familiar with the beautiful phenomenon of the "sun drawing water" (Fig. 86)—sunbeams, that, finding their way through rifts in the clouds, are rendered luminous by the dust in their paths. Many people seem to consider this splendor an excellent weather sign, some insisting that it foretells rain, while others as strongly claim it indicates continued fair. As a matter of fact, it has no significance either way, hence its excellence as a bone of contention.

When there are a number of such rifts the beams of light seem to radiate from the sun like spokes from the hub of a great wheel, or like ribs from the pivot of a giant fan. However, they are practically parallel, for the sun, from which they all come, is 93,000,000 miles away. The seeming divergence is only a perspective illusion, the same as that which makes any long,

CLOUD SPLENDORS 179

FIG. 86. Crepuscular Rays. On the Potomac River

P. E. Budlong, photo.

straight, parallel lines—such, for instance, as the rails on a straight, level track of railway—appear to come closer and closer together with increase of distance.

LIGHTNING

Few things in all Nature so widely range our sensibilities, from thrills of joy over the exquisitely beautiful to abject terror in the face of imminent death, as does the lightning's flash from the heart of the thundercloud.

The story of this wonder meteor—how Franklin showed it to be a form of electric discharge; how, as explained by Simpson, charge after charge following flash after flash is obtained within the cloud by the splitting apart of the bigger drops by the uprushing convection current, the larger portions thus rendered positive accumulating at the base while the negative spray is carried to the top; what curious freaks it plays and marvelous things it does—is delightful in every detail but far too long to include here; for, after all, lightning, whatever its interest and importance, is only a cloud incident.

When the storm is close by it is easy to see that lightning consists of one or more sinuous (not zigzag,

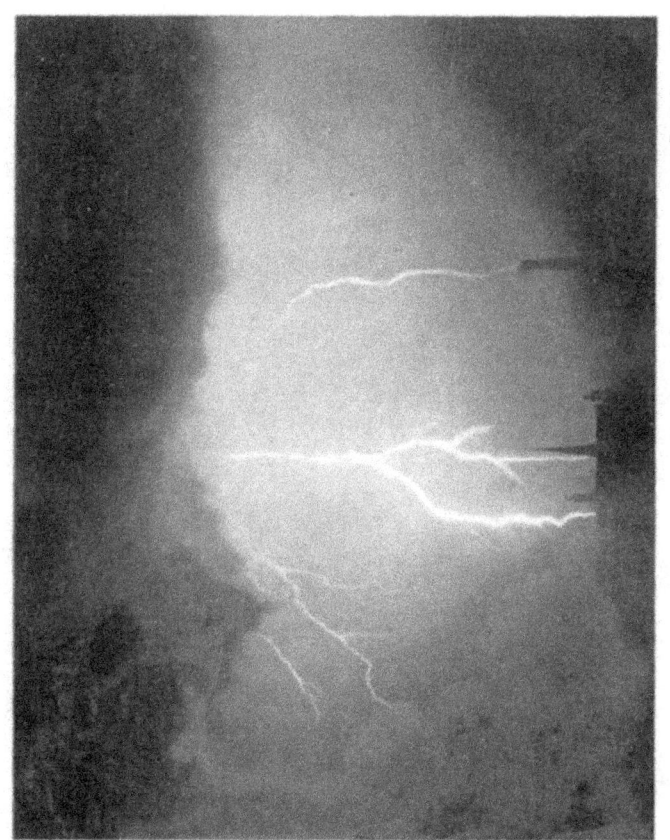

Fig. 87. Lightning. Photographed with a Stationary Camera; Companion to Fig. 88

182   FOGS, CLOUDS AND AVIATION

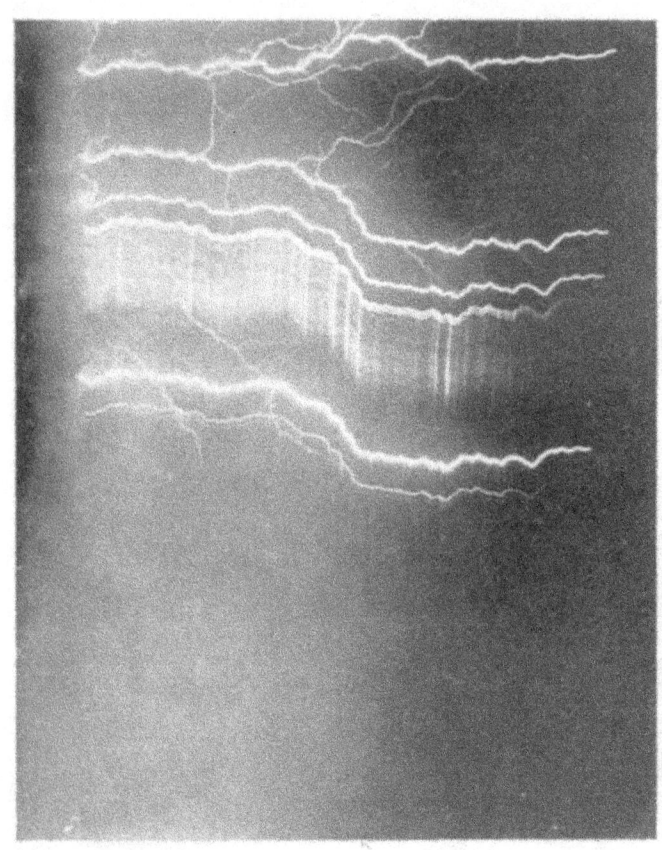

FIG. 88. Lightning. Photographed with a Rotating Camera; Companion to Fig. 87

B. Walter, photo.

CLOUD SPLENDORS 183

F. Ellerman, photo.

FIG. 89. Lightning (Showing also Street Lights of Pasadena). Seen from Mount Wilson, Calif.

Fig. 90. Lightning. Toronto, Canada

as the artist paints it) lines or streaks of vivid white or pink. (Figs. 87 88, 89 and 90.) Often there is one main trunk with a number of branches, all occurring at the same instant, while at other times there are two or more simultaneous disconnected streaks. Frequently the discharge, instead of being all at once, continues flickeringly, giving a series of partial discharges one after another along the same path (Figs. 87 and 88), the first obtained with a stationary camera, the second showing the same discharge spread out with a rotating camera. On rare occasions the lightning appears even stationary, like a glowing wire, during a whole second or more.

THE RAINBOW

Unlike the phenomenon of lightning, the rainbow is all beauty and splendor, with nothing whatever of the appalling—save alone to the physicist who undertakes to explain fully and clearly its every detail—a most difficult task. Perhaps this assertion may seem strange when so many textbooks, even some that are quite elementary, profess to explain the rainbow so simply that a child can understand it. But in this particular nearly all these books have the same fault—

they "explain" beautifully that which does not occur and leave unexplained that which does.

The ordinary rainbow seen in a sheet of water drops —rain, spray, fog—is a group of circular or nearly circular arcs of colors whose common center is on the extension, in the direction of the observer's shadow, of the straight line connecting his eye with the luminous source, which, as everyone knows, is nearly always the sun, but not quite, for once in a while the moon, too, produces a very pretty bow.

Frequently there are two entirely different bows. The inner one, known as the *primary*, with red outer border of about 42° radius, and blue to violet inner border, is much brighter than the larger, or *secondary* bow, of about 50° inner radius, and whose colors occur in the reverse order of those of the primary bow. In addition to these two conspicuous bows one often can see from one to, rarely, half a dozen parallel, colored arcs just inside the primary bow, and a smaller number just outside the secondary bow. These are known as the *supernumerary* bows. Most of these phenomena are shown in Figure 91, copied, by kind permission, from a remarkably fine picture taken by Mr. G. A. Clarke, of Aberdeen, Scotland.

A careful observer will soon see that there is less light (that the clouds look darker) between the two bows than outside the secondary or within the primary; that the colors seen are not always the same; that the band of any given color varies in angular width, even, occasionally, from place to place in the same bow; and that the purity of the colors varies from time to time. As one would naturally suspect, all, or nearly all, these differences depend on the size of the droplets. The greatest contrast, perhaps, is between the brilliant rainbow of the retreating shower and that ill-defined, faintly tinged bow one sometimes sees on a sheet of fog.

THE HALO

As must be obvious to anyone, the cirrus and other very cold clouds nearly always consist of ice crystals. These reflect some of the light that falls upon them; and some of it they transmit, bent, or refracted, as we say, out of its course and split up into all its colors, but always with the red nearest to the source of light. Both the refracted and the reflected light produce various bright patterns properly known as halos.

By refraction we get: the very common ring of 22°

188 FOGS, CLOUDS AND AVIATION

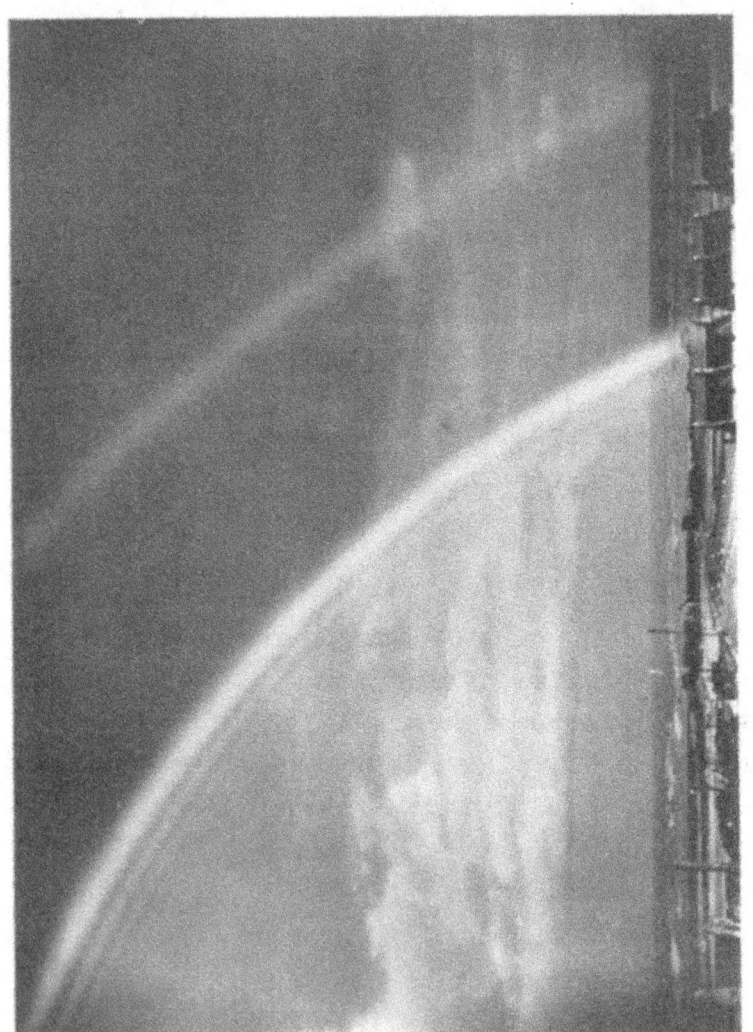

FIG. 91. Rainbow; Primary, Secondary, and Supernumeraries. Seen at Aberdeen, Scotland

G. A. Clarke, photo.

Fig. 92. Halo of 22° and Parhelic Circle in Cirro-Stratus Cloud

Contributed by A. M. Comey.

radius about the sun or moon (Fig. 92); the less frequent ring of 46° radius; the occasional brilliantly colored arc that has its center directly overhead and its convex side next to the sun; and rarely, numerous other splotches and arcs, all more or less distinctly colored, and things of beauty and interest.

By reflection, on the other hand, we get only white or colorless figures; chiefly, the parhelic circle (Fig. 92) that passes through the sun and is parallel to the horizon; and a pillar of light that rises straight up through the sun, much as would its reflection in rippled water if stood on end.

THE CORONA

Thin clouds of water droplets also produce beautiful colored rings about the sun and moon, but usually much smaller than the circles formed by refraction through snow crystals, and with their colors in reverse order; that is, with the red farthest from the source of light instead of nearest to it. These rings, known as coronas, are owing to what the physicist calls diffraction, or, in this case, the bending of the light around the droplets into their shadows. They are most frequently seen about the moon, but may be seen even

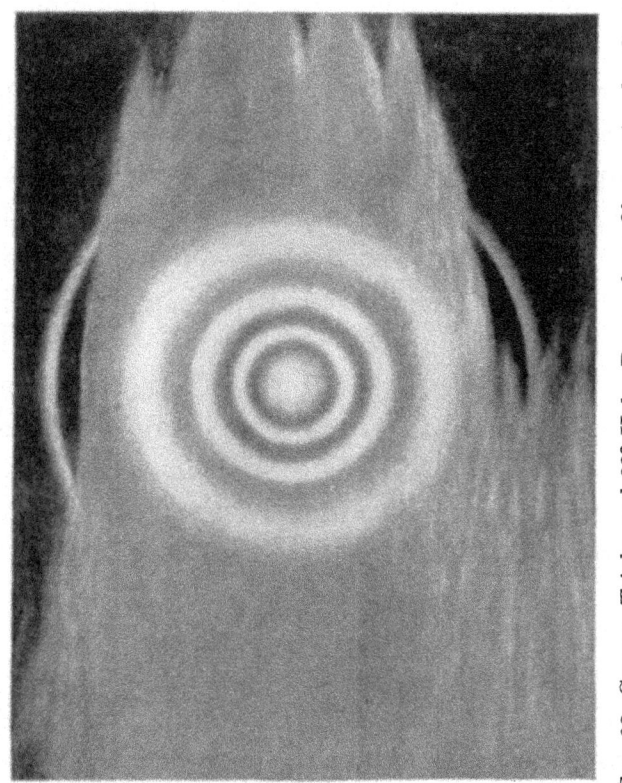

FIG. 93. Corona, Triple, and 22° Halo; Drawn from Observation by G. A. Clarke, Aberdeen, Scotland

more brilliantly, occasionally in a widening series of two or three repetitions of the colors, about the sun, if one will use dark glasses to cut down the glare.

Figure 93, from a drawing by Mr. G. A. Clarke, of Aberdeen, Scotland, shows a magnificent corona and also contains other phenomena observed by him at that place on June 13, 1921. These were: (*a*) The slightly veiled image of the sun; (*b*) an aureole of faintly colored light close to the sun; (*c*) a triple corona in which the radii of the red or outer borders of the three rings were about 6°, 10°, and 16°, respectively; (*d*) iridescence (see below) merged with and extending beyond a portion of the outer coronal ring; (*e*) portions of a fine halo of 22° radius, produced by a background of thin cirrostratus.

CLOUD IRIDESCENCE

Unquestionably the most beautiful thing in all the heavens is a magnificent display of iridescent clouds—numerous splotches among the cirrocumuli, or other high type, and borders of thin lenticular altostrati and altocumuli, of gorgeous opalescent rose pinks, emerald greens, and other colors, randomly mixed and covering a large part of the sky 15° to 30° from the sun.

It can be fully explained (being only fragments of giant coronas due to unusually small droplets), but only in the language of the physicist and symbols of the mathematician. Its beauty, however, can be enjoyed by all, and whoever looks at the heavens for anything should watch most frequently and carefully for the glorious apparition of the iridescent cloud.

BIBLIOGRAPHY

Anyone especially interested in clouds will find several, if not all, of the following worth reading:

LEY, W. CLEMENT, "Cloudland," London, 1894, xiv, 208, pp.; 8 vo. (A study on the structure and characters of the clouds.)

CLAYTON, H. HELM, "Observations made at the Blue Hill Meteorological Observatory—Discussion of the Cloud Observations," Cambridge 1896, 269–500 pp.; 4to. (*Annals of the Astronomical Observatory of Harvard College*, v. 30, pt. 4.)

CLAYDEN, ARTHUR W., "Cloud Studies," London, 1905, xiii, 184 pp.; 8vo.

VINCENT, J., "Atlas des Nuages," Bruxelles, 1907, 29 pp.; folio. (*Annales de l'Observatoire Royale de Belgique, Nouvelle Série. Annales Météorologiques.*)

LOISEL, JULIEN, "Atlas Photographique des Nuages," 2d ed., Paris, 1912 folio. (20 cloud photographs.)

NEUHAUS, E., "Die Wolken," Zurich, 1914, 48 pp.; 30 cloud photographs, 4to. (Use of clouds in local forecasting.)

TAFFARA, L., "Le Nubi," Rome, 1917, 67 pp.; 4to. (50 good cloud photographs; details of cloud observing and photographing.)

CLARKE, G. A., "Clouds," London, 1920, xvi, 136 pp., 12 mo. (Forms, causes, distribution, and weather significance; many excellent illustrations.)

SCHERESCHEWSKY, PH., AND WEHRLÉ, PH., "Les Systèmes Nuageux," Paris, Office National Météorologique, 1923, xvi, 77 pp., with album of charts and album of pictures; 4to. (Relations of cloud systems to weather.)

CAVE, C. J. P., "Clouds and weather phenomena," Cambridge, University Press, 1926. (For artists and other lovers of Nature; 47 good cloud pictures.)

HUMPHREYS, W. J., "Fogs and Clouds," Williams & Wilkins, Waverly Press, Baltimore, 1926.

INDEX

Advection fog, 26
Air, how cooled below dew point, 7
AITKEN, HENRY, 12
AITKEN, JOHN, 12, 14, 41
Altocumulus, 71
    Evaporation of, on cooling, 78
Altostratus, 79
Annual amount of precipitation, 1
Anvil cloud, 145
ARISTOPHANES, 39
Atmosphere, why not saturated, 157
Aviation and cloud:
    altocumulus, 79
    altostratus, 81
    cirrocumulus, 71
    cirrostratus, 63
    cirrus, 62
    cumulus, 110
    nimbostratus, 91
    stratocumulus, 82
Aviation and fog: 37
    advection, 37, 38
    radiation, 37

Banner cloud, 136
Base of cloud sheet, why at common level, 165
BENTLEY, W. A., 155
Billow cloud, 120
Boa cloud, 138

Cap cloud, 141
CAVE, C. J. P., 195

Cirrocumulus, 63
Cirrostratus, 62
    Evidence of usually being snow, 63
Cirrus, 46
    Evidence of usually being snow, 61
    Why no clouds above, 169
CLARKE, G. A., 186, 192, 194
CLAYDEN, ARTHUR W., 194
CLAYTON, H. HELM, 194
Cloud and fog, distinction between, 6, 19
Cloud droplets, rate of fall of, 158
    Size of, 159
Cloudiness, level of maximum, 166
    level of minimum, 169
    variation of, with latitude, 174
Cloud material, 154
Clouds as weather signs, 175
    formation and dissipation of factors controlling, 4
    formed by expansional cooling, 8
    formed by mixing of different masses of air, 7
    height of, measuring, 163
    relation to latitude, 171
    relation to season, 171
    increase of velocity with height, 174
    iridescent, 192
    relation of type to latitude, 171
    to season, 171
    thickness of, 172

198 INDEX

velocities of, 174
why base at common level, 165
why they float, 157
Condensation, 5
  first on hygroscopic nuclei, 17
  discovery of nuclei of, 11
  nuclei of, 11
Cooling of air below dew point, 6
  by contact, 6
  by expansion, 7
  by mixing, 7
Corona, 190
COULIER, P. J., 11
Counting nuclei, 14
Crepuscular rays, 178
Crest cloud, 130
Cumulonimbus, 110
Cumulus, 91
Cumulus boa, 138
Curdled sky, 71

Dew, deposition of, 5
Dew point, 5
  how air is cooled below, 6
Distinction between fog and cloud, 6, 19

ELLIOT, MARIABELLA, 44
Evaporation, 2
  rate of, 2

False cirrus, 110
Fire cumulus, 109
Fog, advection, 26
  black, 31
  caused by radiation, 7
  city, 31
  dry, 26
  how prevented by clouds, 21
    by wind, 21
  ice, 31
  land, 31
  number of particles of, 33
  pea-soup, 31
  quantity of water in, 31
  radiation, 23
  sea, 31
  size of particles of, 33
  summer, 21
  valley, 21
  wet, 26
  where and how formed, 20
  winter, 23
Fog and cloud, distinction between, 6, 19
  essential factors in formation of, 10
Formation and dissipation of clouds, chief factors controlling, 4
Fractocumulus, 92
Fractostratus, 117
FRANKLIN, BENJAMIN, 180
Frost smoke, 23, 31
Funnel cloud, 145

Halo, 187
Heights of clouds, measuring, 163
  relation to latitude, 171
  to season, 170
Helm bar, 135
Helmet cloud, 135
Hoarfrost, formation of, 6

INDEX

HOWARD LUKE, 40, 41, 42, 45, 89
HUMPHREYS, W. J., 195

Ionized air, condensation in, 11
Iridescent cloud, 192

KELVIN, LORD, 12

LAMARCK, 40
LAVOISIER, 42
Lenticular cloud, 123
LEY, W. CLEMENT, 194
Lightning, 180
LOISEL, JULIEN, 194
LONGFELLOW, 1

Mackerel sky, 71
Mammatocumulus, 145
Mares' tails, 47
Maximum cloudiness, levels of, 166
Minimum cloudiness, levels of, 169

NEUHAUS, E., 194
Nimbus, 89
Non-ionized clean air, condensation in, 11
Nuclei, condensation, 11
   counting, 14
   origin and nature of, 16

Pitchers, sweating of, 6
Precipitation, annual amount of, 1

Quantity of water in fog, 31

Rainbow, 185
   primary, 186
   secondary, 186
   supernumerary, 186
Raindrops, relative sizes of, 163
Rain, how produced, 159
Riffle cloud, 135

Saturation, 3
Scarf cloud, 141
SCHERESCHEWSKY, PH., 194
Scud, 90
SHAKESPEARE, 39
SHELLEY, v, 1, 178
SIMPSON, G. C., 180
Size of cloud droplets, 159
   fog particles, 33
   relative, of raindrops, 163
Smog, 31
Snow crystal, shape of, 155
Steaming of rivers and lakes, 23
Stratocumulus, 81
Stratus, 117
Sun drawing water, 178

Table cloth, 130
TAFFARA, L., 194
Temperature, relation to humidity, 5
Thickness of clouds, 172
THURAS, A. L., 32
Tonitro-cirrus, 144
Tornado cloud, 145
Type of clouds, relation to latitude, 171
   relation to season, 171

Vapor, relation of quantity of to temperature, 5
Velo cloud, 117
Velocity, cloud, increase with height, 174
VINCENT, J., 194

Waterspout, 153
Wave cloud, 120
WEHRLÉ, PH., 195
WELLS, P. V., 32
Windrow cloud, 126

www.ingramcontent.com/pod-product-compliance
Lightning Source LLC
LaVergne TN
LVHW041616070426
835507LV00008B/272